MEXICAN
COUNTRY

STYLE

MEXICAN
COUNTRY
STYLE

Karen Witynski

Joe P. Carr

GIBBS·SMITH
PUBLISHER

SALT LAKE CITY

To my mother, Judith M. Simpson, and the memory of my father, Stanley S. Witynski

Text copyright ©1997 by Karen Witynski and Joe P. Carr
Photograph copyrights as noted on page 137

00 99 98 97 5 4 3 2 1

This is a Peregrine Smith Book,
published by
Gibbs Smith, Publisher
P.O. Box 667
Layton, Utah 84041

Designed by Christine Nasser
Edited by Gail Yngve

Printed in Hong Kong

Library of Congress Cataloging-in-Publication Data

Witynski, Karen, 1960–
    Mexican country style / Karen Witynski and Joe P. Carr.
    — 1st ed.
        p.   cm.

    "A Peregrine Smith book,"

    ISBN 0-87905-814-5

    1. Ethnic art in interior decoration. 2. Decoration and ornament,
Rustic — Mexico. 3. Ethnic art — Mexico. I. Carr, Joe P., 1942–   .
NK2115.5.E84W58   1997
747.2'972 — DC21   97-6920
                CIP

Cover: A late nineteenth-century Mexican table with a *sabino* top and turned mesquite legs holds contemporary *hibachis*, ingeniously recycled from Oaxacan license plates. Collection of Karen Witynski and Joe Carr. Photograph by Teresa Harb Diehl.

Title Page: Colonial-style spindled window guard on the Calderella home in El Paso, Texas. Photograph by Gill Kenny.

Table of Contents: A painted altar table with a fluted *faldon*, or skirt, and turned legs holds a green ceramic candelabra from Michoacán. Collection of Ed Holler and Sam Saunders. Photograph by Alexander Vertikoff.

ACKNOWLEDGMENTS

Many dear people contributed generously to this book, sharing their support and enthusiasm. We are grateful first to our friends in Mexico, the craftsmen, antique dealers, and experts who have shared their knowledge and spirited hospitality over the years. A heartfelt thanks to Alicia and Tony Castillo, Jose Martinez, Tony Piraino, Enrique Lopez, David Martinez, Virginia B. de Barrios, Sergio and Bethzi Romero, Marie Pierre-Colle, and Felix Rogelio Lopez.

We wish to express our appreciation to the people who were an integral part of shaping this book. We thank our agent, Betsy Amster, for her expertise, sound advice, and magic touch; our editor, Gail Yngve, for her dedication and support of our vision; art director Christine Nasser for her creative talents; and Dorothy Atcheson and Amy Witynski for their valuable assistance with the manuscript. In addition to research and editing assistance, Amy provided inspiring sisterly "wit" on a daily basis. We also extend our gratitude to production artist Deborah Davis for her attention to detail.

Un mil gracias to our antique-dealer friends for letting us loose among their private collections to document their fine examples of Mexican furniture: Jack Dulaney, Rene Bustamente, Ed Holler, Sam Saunders, Omer Claiborne, Jack and Peggy Calderella, Rick Rosenthal, Harl Dixon, Alex Tschursin, and Joshua Baer.

The following designers have given generously of their time and knowledge: Barbara Pohlman, Carolyn Reichow, Karen Vaughan, Sally Pepin, Annie O'Carroll, Susan Dupépé, Craig Wright, Jackie Morgan, and Laben Wingert. A special word of appreciation to Stephen Brady of Banana Republic for his inspiring innovation.

A special thanks to friends and associates who gave insightful advice and help, among them: Gloria Kay Giffords, Diane Bruce at The Institute of Texan Cultures, Jim Dunlap, Rhonda Gainer, Leo Gomez, Sharon Zelle, Liz Gardner, and Gloria Rios. And to our *amiga* Margo Chavez for her assistance with translations and her network of contacts in Mexico. Also, special *abrazos* to the many photographers who have contributed to this work, especially Teresa Harb Diehl. And to Mariana Yampolsky for her kindness in allowing us to reprint her inspiring photographs in this book.

A special thank you to Ruben Cordova of The Mexican Museum for his continued support and for writing the foreword.

We would also like to thank the following people who hospitably opened their homes and offices to us: James Havard, Ted Turner and Jane Fonda, Morton and Donna Fleischer, Dr. and Mrs. Alfredo Sosa Rojas, Martha Eagan, Vincent Carrozo, Victor DiSuvero and Barbara Windom, Virginia Dwan, Mr. and Mrs. Ramon Fasada, Bart and Brenda Jacobs, Dan and Lynne Gelfman, Jack and Claudia Auger, Lee Nichols, Buffy Birrittella, Jerry and Carolyn Reichow, Rene Bustamente and Ann Miller, Don and Karen Berlanti, Omer and Bunny Claiborne, Richard and Nedra Matteucci, Betty Kaye Gilmore, Michelle Gravelin, Ron and Suzie Dubin, and Rolf and Niltha Gerstner. A very special thank you to Ed Holler and Sam Saunders for their endless hospitality in Mexico.

Finally, our deep appreciation to our families for their constant support: my mother, Judith M. Simpson, and sisters—Amy, Mara, and Jenny Witynski—and to my late father, Stanley S. Witynski, who encouraged our vision for this book years ago; and special thanks to the generous support of Joe P. Carr Sr.

A very special thank you

To Aeromexico
for providing us with air transportation
during our research trips to Mexico.

To the Inn of the Anasazi in Santa Fe, New Mexico,
for providing us with a peaceful and luxurious retreat
while we were on location in the Southwest.

CONTENTS

FOREWORD

The rich cultural legacy of Spain and Mexico in the present-day American Southwest extends back several centuries. This region was explored by the shipwrecked *Cabeza de Vaca* beginning in 1528. The Spanish settled in New Mexico in 1598, in Arizona in 1700, in Texas in 1716, and in California in 1769. This cultural heritage is evident throughout the landscape, from the historic missions to the bright colors and devices of postmodern architecture. Multiculturalism has helped bring about a widespread appreciation of Mexican art, architecture, craft, folklore, music, dance, and food—all of which have been celebrated in numerous publications. Yet *Mexican Country Style* is the first substantial treatment of the rustic, utilitarian furniture, architectural elements, vessels, and accessories whose austere beauty I have long admired.

As a child, I spent many spellbound hours meditating on such objects, including hand-wrought tools, ingenious gate latches, and hand-adzed battened doors. My first intense aesthetic experience was afforded by the interlaced *latias* of an adobe house built by my great-grandfather on his ranch in the mountains of New Mexico. As I gazed with awe at the branches that had been stained a dazzling turquoise blue, I thought of the hands that had shaped them almost a century before. I also admired the massive vigas in the adjacent ranch-style house built by my grandfather. Some years later, I helped a brother fashion paneling out of the remnants of a wooden fence that had been abandoned for decades. The wood had been bleached by the sun, stained by pigments in the earth, and worn by erosion, causing its grain to stand out in dark, dramatic relief against its blue-gray surface. It was as pleasing to the hand as it was to the eye.

In a world filled with disposable products, plastics, and far too many objects of dubious workmanship, it is pleasurable and reassuring to contemplate works that have served faithfully for generations, bearing the marks of time. Such objects evoke the rhythms of rural life from which they originated. Time-honored artistic traditions and modes of expression underlay their design. Their years of service as ritual and utilitarian objects also helped to shape them. Some show the impact of tools, the deposits left by organic substances, layers of paint applied by previous generations of users, or the wear caused by countless admiring caresses.

Mexican Country Style celebrates the widespread appreciation of this richly expressive style with great artistry. Its pages reveal how these pieces have become cherished elements in the homes and offices of artists, decorators, anthropologists, businessmen, film stars, fashion designers, antique dealers, and collectors.

Since its founding in 1975, The Mexican Museum has been dedicated to showing the entire history of Mexican and Chicano art, from the great indigenous civilizations to the cutting edge of contemporary art. As we prepare to break ground for our new building in the Yerba Buena district of San Francisco, we look forward to the vast increase in exhibition space that will enable us to put a substantial portion of our 10,000 objects on permanent display. We take pride in our collection of country objects, which will always have their rightful place in the panorama of Mexican art and culture.

Ruben C. Cordova, Curator

The Mexican Museum

INTRODUCTION

FOR DECADES, MEXICO'S COUNTRYSIDE HAS STARTLED OUR SENSES WITH THE RICH FLAVORS OF its tradition-bound world. As antique dealers and designers, we first became acquainted with Mexican furniture and architectural elements in the early 1970s as we traveled throughout the states of Zacatecas, San Luis Potosí, and Jalisco, collecting textiles, masks, and folk art for our then New Mexico gallery. Charmed by the character and ingenuity of the Mexican people, we were drawn to the rugged, romantic beauty of their architecture and the soulful antiquity of their handcrafted elements.

As we became more and more familiar with the everyday routines of Mexican life, we found ourselves curious about the markings and textures that decades of time and wear had left on the indigenous furnishings and objects we had discovered—character marks that were alive with history, color, and personality. Very simply, they fired our imaginations. The stories behind these pieces were the inspiration for this book. Our twenty-five-plus years of buying, collecting, restoring, and selling Mexican antiques have been a constant learning experience, rewarding us with surprises at every turn, and bringing us closer to the vitality of the people of Mexico and their colorful heritage.

By the mid-1970s, our quest for Mexican country pieces had become all-consuming and kept us in constant motion between our Guadalajara studio and our New Mexico gallery. Our

A palm-lined driveway is protected by a weathered pair of grand entrance doors. Lake Pátzcuaro home of Ed Holler and Sam Saunders.

Authors Karen Witynski and Joe Carr inspect a painted trunk from Michoacán at an antique flea market in Mexico.

Opposite: One of a matching pair of painted pine scalloped benches was found in Zacatecas. El Paso Imports Collection.

first buying trips became adventures as we wound our way by bus and burro through coastal villages and old colonial mining towns, bumping alongside sugarcane fields and down narrow cobblestoned streets in search of simple, robust country tables, workbenches, storage trunks, corral gates, and old, heavy doors. We had never expected to see such diversity. The variety in style, design, and shape of the utilitarian vessels and carved wooden objects we found was astounding. From milking stools shaped like animals to grain-measure boxes and sculptural sugar molds, the pieces were like mirrors reflecting a rich local history as well as the ingenuity of the hands that made them. We enjoyed learning about the importance of these mundane artifacts, all essential elements of daily existence that were nevertheless considered valuable enough to be worthy of creative expression.

Coauthor Joe Carr discovers a unique table in the marketplace.

Serendipity brought us to ranchos, coffee plantations, and bustling open-air markets, where we were drawn to well-worn display surfaces revealing rich patinas and wood grains. Sometimes, underneath mounds of papayas and rows of candied limes, we discovered stunning turned-leg tables or charming old prep tables whose myriad chop marks evidenced decades of use. No single purchase has given us more lasting pleasure than the bright blue market table we found in Zacatecas, shrouded beneath a floral oilcloth—a wonderful reminder that village markets provide bountiful displays not only of the local harvests but of their time-honored furnishings as well.

Over the years, our love for the thriving market experience has sparked a ritual that we live by religiously to this day. No matter what town or village

we alight on, the first stop on our buying trips—sometimes even direct from the airport—is the *mercado*. There we can instantly immerse ourselves in the rhythms of Mexico, absorbing the vitality and openness of the people, and rejuvenating our spirits with the riot of colors, sights, and sounds. As we search the marketplace for antiques, we also buy our daily survival supplies—armfuls of lilies for the hotel room and avocados and fresh-baked *bolillos* for midday snacks, not to mention black peppercorns and chiles to refresh our stocks back home. Then we often plant ourselves in the center of the action at a market-stall restaurant to take in the magic. While munching our favorite *gorditas*, washed down with *agua de jamaica*, a ruby-red blended drink made from hibiscus blossoms, we might spot a unique kitchen object or handcrafted element right there in use at the restaurant. The atmosphere at the marketplace is so conducive to gossip and conversation that asking

questions is very easy. It is there that we practice our Spanish and learn more about the functional objects of everyday Mexican life.

The antiques kept us company on our drives back from Mexico; then they found their way into our homes, blending as easily with the adobe architecture of New Mexico as with our more contemporary home in Texas. Their simplicity and rich hardwoods added depth and character to our rooms, becoming our favored pieces to live with, both because of their visual appeal and because they inspired fond thoughts of Mexico.

The pieces soon became an integral part of our design work, too, as we placed unusual architectural fragments and utilitarian objects in our interior design projects. From mesquite-carved beams and window lintels to jail doors and coffee mortars, we found new homes for our unusual finds where they were welcomed for their hearty proportions and well-worn presence. Many of our salvaged discoveries—sometimes half sculpture/half furniture—provided innovative artistic accents that defied conventional design themes. We found that our collection of folk art, textiles, and ceramics played well with the Mexican antiques. Hand-carved ox yokes held court with Oaxacan *huipiles*, while Day of the Dead sugar skulls sat atop painted Mexican trunks. The gallery's unusual juxtapositions sought colorful comments from visiting clients. We soon found that our customers were as intrigued as we were with the Mexican objects, and they shared our curiosity to know more about the objects' origins.

Although Mexican country elements are inseparable from the country itself, we found it perplexing that the history of Mexican architecture, arts, textiles, and even folk toys has been exhaustively documented, while the story of Mexican country antiques has been virtually ignored. Writers on Mexican furnishings have limited their focus to Spanish Colonial—the more ornate, European-influenced styles. But the

Above: A grouping of corral hinges, or *pivote de rejas*, are carved from solid mesquite, and form a decorative montage on an aging wall. Collection of Karen Witynski and Joe Carr.

An old sugar mold, or *molde de azucar*, features conical-shaped indentations for making brown sugar.

Opposite: A contemporary setting combines a coffee mortar filled with gourds and a hand-carved sugar mold. Painting, *Agave,* by Mara Beth Witynski.

A Mexican harvest table and chairs add a splash of color to this contemporary kitchen. Collection of Virginia Dwan.

indigenous popular furniture of Mexico has an equally rich history—one that has hitherto been almost unknown.

Lacking a comprehensive published work on the subject, we were prompted to piece together our own resource library to share with friends and customers. In Mexico, we gathered photographs and researched details wherever possible, traveling to visit public and private collections on both sides of the border. Thanks to the helpful assistance of Mexican book

Pine trunks on stands from Chihuahua, once used for storing clothing, share this hallway with a James Havard painting.

Below: A Zacatecas table leg shows layers of crackled paint.

and antiques dealers, we acquired reference books, periodicals, and museum monographs (all in Spanish) that had marginal references to the simpler country styles, most notably, the Franz Meyer Museum in Mexico City, the Acapulco Historical Museum—Fuerte de San Diego, the Museum of Guadalajara, the Pátzcuaro Regional Museum, and a charming display of furniture in the upper story of Santo Domingo Church in Oaxaca. These locations and others afforded us the opportunity to get close to the country pieces whose roots we were seeking to unearth. Often we made surprise discoveries of old country pieces while visiting small colonial hotels scattered throughout Mexico.

We have been especially fortunate in the friends we have made, for through their eyes and stories we have been privileged to see and learn about the antiques of Mexico. Fascinating and amusing hours have been

A simple Chihuahua bench keeps company with a collection of *retablos* and tin frames. Santa Fe home of Ron and Suzie Dubin.

spent with *carpinteros*, farmers, salvage and antique dealers, and other enterprising individuals as we examined old relics—doors, gates, altar tables, *armarios*, or armoires, and trunks—and learned the subtleties of the local hardwoods, construction methods, hardware styles, and original uses. We gradually acquired the answers to our countless questions, often over family meals or while we watched children's street soccer games.

We were inspired also by the pioneering atmosphere surrounding the beginnings of this market and the creative synergy among the handful of dealers in the border towns of El Paso, Nogales, and Laredo. This innovative network allowed us the pleasure of being surrounded by people who shared our vision and belief in the appeal of these pieces. We never would have imagined, especially during our early days of unloading trucks at the border, that our early efforts would have attracted a phenomenal interest in the pieces that came out of those dusty trucks. Over a few years, it has evolved into a virtual phenomenon—an industry that, in addition to the antiques, now includes accessories and a number of fine reproductions made from reclaimed wood and original architectural fragments.

The effort involved in importing these pieces and the energy consumed in their restoration, marketing, and sales have had remarkable results. Mexican country style is fast enriching the American design scene as it is now accessible in every corner of the country. Although artists and collectors have been enjoying and living with Mexican antiques and accents for decades, it is the last ten years that have witnessed the most meteoric rise in their popularity.

In early 1990, we opened a second gallery to accommodate the increased interest—especially in the larger pieces—from designers, architects, and homeowners.

Transcending their Southwest origins, many of these vigas, doors, and gates have been shipped to New York, Rhode Island, Florida, and Illinois,

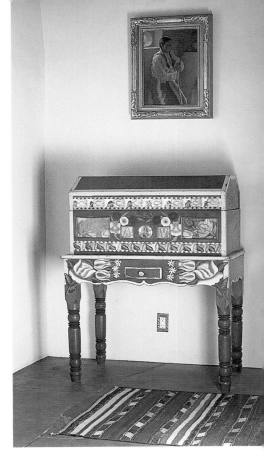

Once a trousseau of a Puebla bride, this brightly decorated Puebla chest highlights a bedroom corner of the Berlanti home in Santa Fe. Interior design by Visions Design Group.

Following page: Contemporary stone spheres are reminiscent of the natural stone geodes used in outdoor courtyard spaces by renowned Mexican architect Ricardo Legoretta. Colonial courtyard of Ed Holler and Sam Saunders' Morelia home.

A unique example of a
Zacatecas *gran armario* on
a *zapata*, or shoe base. Its
distinguishing feature includes
dental molding on lower portion
of the *copete*, complex raised
panels on the front and sides,
and a cutout *faldon*, or skirt,
that resembles those on early
colonial pieces.

Opposite top: Painted mesquite
chair with carved back and
front rung.

Opposite below: A combination
cabinet and table featuring
raised-panel doors, delicately
turned legs from Zacatecas, and
an intricate cutout design under
the skirt on both front and sides.
Both pieces were made at the
same time; however, they are
not attached.

All pieces on these two pages
are from the El Paso Imports
Collection.

finding themselves at home in a variety of settings—from simple country retreats in Montana to illustrious New York lofts to hotels, gardens, and specialty stores across the country. Beginning their lives in marketplaces, ranchos, and workshops as the cornerstones of cultural traditions involving family, religion, and devoted celebrations, these relics of real life have evolved gracefully over time and have transcended borders and cultural boundaries to transform today's contemporary spaces, taking root in a variety of indoor and outdoor environments in the United States and Mexico.

As our world grows increasingly complex and technology distances us from our own traditional ways, it makes sense that we are drawn to the qualities manifest in Mexican antiques. There's no denying the appeal of handcrafted wood. We believe in the beauty and artistic power of the designs, in their lasting value, and in the skill of their creators. The character they bear from the effects of time, weather, and touch reassures us, perhaps tapping into a distant longing for simpler times when craftsmen took pride both in the quality and the sturdiness of their work.

Still, though Mexican country antiques are ever-present in our homes and stores, they sometimes elude an accurate identity or are misunderstood, getting mislabeled in magazines and in discussions. Perhaps owing to the lack of resource material about them, people have been left with no choice but to categorize the pieces as primitive, ethnic, or southwestern. Thus, this book offers the first comprehensive look at the timeless beauty and versatility of Mexico's indigenous styles and their newfound presence in modern and country homes in the United States. It is the first book also to document the style from its rural origins to its contemporary manifestations. In the following pages, we introduce a variety of styles—many from never-before-seen private collections—and examine details on regional differences, woods, restoration, and original uses.

Our fascination and enthusiasm for Mexico has led us on an incredible journey. We have connected to the strength, imagination, and beauty of the country's handwrought objects, taking great pleasure in seeing them in their original contexts—such as in workshops, coffee plantations, homes, and haciendas, and in the midst of processions at Christmas and *Semana Santa*. We have relished living with them on a daily basis and have watched as the antiques have been reinvented and adapted to new contexts since an

A painted cypress bench with scalloped seat front and backrest offers a quiet spot for rest or reflection under Don and Karen Berlanti's adobe portal.

Opposite: Entrance to the Carrozo house in Santa Fe is gained by large Mexican *portones*, or doors, from the state of Durango, which open into an aspen-filled inner courtyard.

entire industry has evolved from the influences of these old-country elements. We applaud this recent momentum and look forward to a continuing celebration of the rich heritage of Mexican country antiques.

Delighted to share the discoveries from our pilgrimages into the past, we are also pleased to share our expertise and passionate enjoyment of Mexican country style. We hope *Mexican Country Style* will inspire design ideas and help identify styles as well as provide a source of visual pleasure for collectors of antiques, those interested in interior design, or those who are simply fascinated with Mexico.

ORIGINS

FOR CENTURIES, THE MEXICAN CRAFTSMAN HAS INSTINCTIVELY COMBINED BEAUTY WITH function, using the materials provided by nature to create furniture, culinary vessels, architectural elements, implements, and religious objects. The elements of the countryside reflect Mexico's wildly diverse landscape and her pre-Columbian, European, and Indian influences. From Aguascalientes to Zacatecas, Morelia to Oaxaca, this land of extreme contrasts includes fertile valleys, tropical forests, arid deserts, high mountain places, and deep canyons. Dotting the landscape are the old colonial mining cities and rural villages where natives still weave and make pottery.

For thousands of years, Mexican craftsmen have been making use of the earth, stone, and wood of their native regions to create functional and noble elements. From adobe dwellings and stone walls to bamboo fences and wooden furnishings, their designs are products of their locations and centuries of tradition influenced by the dual Spanish and Indian heritage of the country as well as the practical demands of daily life. Like their pre-Spanish Conquest ancestors, most of the *campesinos*, or country people, are artists, making objects of great beauty from whatever is at hand: gourds for water storage, maguey fiber for rope and bags, clay vessels for cooking and storage, wood objects for use in the fields or home.

The Mexican people's relationship with their natural environment has always been one of harmony, and their functional elements are filled with ingenuity. Even today, creative use is made

An early chip-carved table from Oaxaca is covered with glass spheres and *santos* in the Morelia home of Ed Holler and Sam Saunders.

San José is the patron saint of carpenters, and since 1702, his feast day has been celebrated in Mexico City's Church of San Francisco. His image is present in many workshops and homes. Courtesy Ray Pearson and Gloria Kay Giffords, *The Art of Private Devotion:* Retablo *Painting of Mexico*, Meadows Museum.

Opposite: A lacquered trunk from Olinalá sits atop a cypress table with intricately carved apron. Claiborne Gallery, Santa Fe, New Mexico.

of all materials, with many elements being recycled for new uses. One can find *hibachis* and flower planters made from old license plates, for example. In the countryside, young boys sport palm-leaf raincoats, and children play with cane whistles and slingshots of sisal fiber near fences of live organ-pipe cactus. Roofs are layered with rye stalks or dried maguey cactus leaves, and animal watering troughs are carved from stone.

Ancient Mayan leader Huehuetlalli gave these words of admonishment:

Take care of the things of the earth,
Do something, cut wood, work the soil, plant the cactus, plant the maguey.
You will have to drink, to eat, to dress,
Thus you will stride,
Thus they will speak of you, praise you,
Thus, you will be known, thus you will stand on your feet, be real.

After the Spanish Conquest in 1521, the culture of Mexico became a mixture of native and Spanish elements. Although craftsmen in the cities adopted the materials, techniques, and ideas introduced by the Spaniards, they also preserved their own indigenous methods.

During the 300 years of Spanish rule, the furniture styles of the cities varied considerably from those of the countryside. While the styles were equally worthy and depended in all cases on the potential functions of the pieces, the availability of natural resources, and the skill of the craftsmen, city craftsmen generally had better tools and produced furniture of greater sophistication. Still, the rural workshops created equally interesting pieces, especially as country craftsmen were able to exercise more artistic license. A significant factor for the *carpinteros*, or carpenters, in the colonial cities was the role that the government guild system played.

After the establishment of the colonial government, artisan guilds were formed. An ordinance was granted to the guild of carpenters, carvers, joiners, and lutemakers by the Noble City of Mexico on August 30, 1568, and was confirmed by the *audiencia* on October 26 of the same year. In part, the ordinance controlled the quality of the objects sold and established qualifications for guild membership.

Guild laws were generally enforced within largely populated areas. As one moved out to the more casual environment of the countryside, however, where pieces were sometimes commissioned for municipal offices,

churches, and the like, the laws were sometimes not applicable to local *carpinteros* or were difficult to enforce.

Throughout the rural landscape, *carpinteros* in provincial towns and villages worked without guild constraints and thus crafted elements from their own traditions and resources. On occasion, they even interpreted Spanish-influenced styles that had made their way naturally from the cities

to the countryside—through families moving to the country or storing old, broken pieces in rural barns, say. Such interpretations were, of course, simplified or streamlined to be practical and durable in rural settings. Carved lyre legs became sturdy A-frame legs; ornately carved panels on armoires were streamlined into handsome flat-panel styles, lathe-turned spindles on cupboards were sometimes simplified into slats.

Unlike the more formal environments of the cities, furniture had a multipurpose life in the countryside; it was shared by many and used for a variety of functions in myriad locations. Whether needed for marketplace displays, home or workshop use, or religious celebrations and community fiestas, one piece might be used for every setting and moved back and forth according to its owner's activities.

On the other hand, the furniture produced for the wealthy *hacendados*, or hacienda owners, and government officials was usually styled according to what was popular in Europe at the time. The furniture commonly used in sixteenth-century Mexico was primarily Spanish in style, though it acquired individual characteristics as it was adapted by native craftsmen. In Mexico City and Puebla, carpenters copied Spanish designs, mirroring the styles that were in vogue there, including intricately carved armoires and lyre-leg refectory tables in walnut, cedar, cypress, and mesquite. Trained guild craftsmen were commissioned to produce furniture and elaborate altar pieces for churches and government buildings.

As a result of colonial trade with China and Japan, Mexican furniture designs also showed Oriental influences, characterized in the use of lacquerware and marquetry. Abundantly produced in Mexico until the nineteenth century, lacquered tables, wardrobes, and chests were popularly traded along the Chihuahua trail and made their way to the northern trade fairs reaching as far north as Santa Fe, New Mexico. Mexican lacquered-furniture elements, which after the Spanish Conquest were produced predominately in the

Above: This mesquite tree shades a work area on a ranch in the state of Hidalgo. Courtesy *Arquitectura Vernácula en México*, Editorial Trillas.

Below: An excellent example of an early colonial mesquite table that has a large locking drawer and turned stretchers and legs. Collection of Rick Rosenthal.

Opposite: An old colonial table once used in a convent by nuns as a re-dressing table for their carved saints is now at home with eclectic treasures in the contemporary *sala* of Ed Holler and Sam Saunders.

states of Michoacán and Chiapas, have appeared on many estate inventories in New Mexico and its surrounding areas. Also traded in substantial numbers with the United States were the brightly painted, lacquered, six-board chests. Most significant were the colorful bridal chests from Olinalá, Guerrero, and the polychromed chests and boxes from around the Lake Pátzcuaro region in Michoacán.

Following Mexico's independence in 1821, the colonial guilds were dismantled, opening up many more creative interpretations and allowing for much more variety and affordability. Overall, the designs emanating from the colonial period didn't disappear. Yet without ordinances dictating standard sizes, designs weren't so labor intensive and became more universally affordable. Lighter woods were used, too, which made the pieces easier to transport, and the resulting scaled-down, less ornate designs made pieces more versatile.

The woods used in Mexican country furniture were predominately mesquite, *sabino*, or Mexican cypress, pine, heart pine, Spanish cedar, *parota*, and occasionally walnut, elm, cottonwood, and ash. Mesquite, one of the most durable hardwoods, was widely used as it was found from the Sonoran desert all the way down the west coast of Durango, Aguascalientes, Jalisco, Nayarit, and then inland to the Hidalgo/Guanajuato area. It is nonexistent in higher altitudes, however.

Both mesquite and *sabino* were sought for their strength and natural ability to repel insects. *Sabino*, which ranges in color from golden brown to butterscotch, was found throughout high-plateau areas near marshes or along riverbeds, primarily in the states of Mexico, Jalisco, Puebla, Tlaxcala, Nayarit, and Guerrero. Equally strong, heart pine, or *corazón de yarín*, is a reddish brown hardwood, stronger than the more common pine. It is found in northern Mexico to Michoacán, Zacatecas, and Mexico City. Along the coast of Colima and Guerrero, *parota* was widely available.

Carpentry during the colonial era required hearty craftsmen, as it was much more physical work than it is today. The simple act of getting stock required chopping down trees with axes, or *hachas*, then dragging them by mule or ox to a work area where they would be cut into slabs by pit saws—long saws with handles at each end operated by two people, one below in a dugout pit and one on top. After the wood had properly dried over time, it

Next to a mesquite table, a woman waves a clay brazier containing burning incense over an offering of food and drink. Since ancient times, *copal* has been used as incense in sacred rites. Courtesy Editorial Minutiae Mexicana, *A Guide to Mexican Witchcraft*.

Opposite: An adobe house in the Chiapas highlands adds color to the rugged beauty of the Mexican countryside. Courtesy *Arquitectura Vernácula en México*, Editorial Trillas.

was cut into smaller slabs and then sized and dressed—smoothed with an adz. It was only at this point that it was ready to be crafted into furniture.

When fashioning furniture, carpenters used augers for drilling holes. Or, in some instances, if specific tools weren't available, they heated iron rods to burn holes into the wood. *Escoplos*, or chisels, were used to make the mortises and tenons, and an array of gouges and knives were used for carving decorative elements. In more sophisticated workshops, lathes were at

hand for turning table legs and spindles. Craftsmen also used carpenters' benches with long vices to plane edges squarely for quality joinery. This process persisted throughout colonial times and into independence, as it was not until the advent of lumber mills in the latter part of the nineteenth century that woodworking became simpler.

As with any trade or craft, there are various levels of skill and operation. Certainly, if one were to look at the full range of artistry that took place in the realm of carpentry, three levels of furniture-making could be identified: first, the highly skilled master craftsmen who were guild members; second, the craftsmen who had trained through apprenticeships or who learned techniques through non-guild family members working outside of the cities; and third, the provincial villager who was not officially trained but who had great skills and worked in many trades, wearing the hats of carpenter, when necessary, or perhaps the village *santero*, or saint maker, or cobbler.

Many furnishing and agricultural implements were fashioned from materials at hand and transformed through the simplest processes—reeds and rushes woven into mats, chair seats, or baskets; tree stumps carved into stools and mortars; planks hand-adzed for doors and tables; local stone chiseled into vessels for animal feed or bases for portal beams.

Scallops and spindles decorate the cornice of a *trastero*.

Opposite: *Cocina Poblana*, by Eduardo Pingret, features a look at a Puebla kitchen in the late 1800s. Courtesy National Museum of History, Chapultepec Castle, Mexico.

FURNITURE AREAS

The major furniture-producing areas were the ones with the highest populations, such as Mexico City, Puebla, and Guadalajara. Moving out toward the countryside, significant regions included Pátzcuaro, Morelia, Uruapan, San Luis Potosí, and Olinalá.

Although certain styles of furniture were produced throughout Mexico—the ubiquitous ranch table, for example—like most countries with strong furniture traditions, if you look closely, regional differences become apparent. Much to the delight of collectors and designers, this is the case with Mexican antiques.

An intricately chip-carved
Spanish cedar bench from
Oaxaca adds depth and function
to this grand hallway.

In the northern state of Chihuahua, furniture is usually made from pine, is fairly minimal in design, and is almost always painted, as it helps preserve the wood. Panels can be flat or raised, and the favored decoration is a scalloped or cutout *copete*, or crest, attached to the top of *armarios*, or armoires, *roperos*, or wardrobes, and *trasteros*, or cupboards. Scalloping is also occasionally added to the backsplash of sideboards, shelves, or the bottom of storage pieces. The Mennonite communities that settled in northern Mexico migrated from Canada in the early 1920s with government grants to farm the land. With them, they brought a legacy of carpentry traditions from Germany and Russia, and excelled in joinery and lathe work — hence, the prolific use of spindles and turned legs in this region.

South of Chihuahua in Zacatecas, benches are decorated with undulating scallop designs resembling waves. Panels in cabinets tend to be raised and come in a variety of designs besides those that are simply square-raised. Tables usually have signature-design cutout braces under the skirt and in each corner.

In the nearby states of Jalisco, Aguascalientes, and Guanajuato, the styles are much heavier and are crafted from the hardwoods mesquite and *sabino*. These styles are also more influenced by the colonial furniture traditions of the seventeenth and eighteenth centuries. In the southern state of Oaxaca, chip-carving and gouge-carving decorate the benches and cabinets, while tables are generally made from cypress, Spanish cedar, and pine. Long, slender tables with A-frame legs and stretchers are common, as are single-slab tabletops. Chip-carving styles are also very prolific in Michoacán's Lake Pátzcuaro region where the majority of pieces are pine, as this area has large reserves of pine forest.

Over the years, the country furniture of Mexico has evolved from its humble beginnings and varied origins, and helped to lay the foundation for a now-thriving industry through its growth.

ELEMENTS

WHEREVER MEXICAN ELEMENTS ARE FOUND—HIGH IN MOUNTAIN VILLAGES, FAR OFF THE beaten track in fertile farmland communities, on ranchos, or in old colonial towns—they are surrounded by the routines of everyday life. Sparking images of generation after generation, the elements raise questions that often remain a mystery. "Who made this? What was it used for?" Imaginations conjure the countryside—the simplified traditions of family activities, work, and celebration—that surrounded these elements and gave them history and a sense of place.

Indeed, the Mexican people have an innate sense of order and composition that proliferates in everything from the carefully arranged fruits and vegetables of the marketplace, to the sidewalk patterns made of stone, to the homes proudly displaying carefully crafted objects and furniture. From old ranch tables, benches, and cupboards to carved wooden vessels and sugar molds, Mexican country elements are alive with timeless character and ingenuity.

Mexico's interior furnishings, implements, and architectural accents—whether found in humble *casitas* or comfortable country homes—reflect the availability of the natural resources in their local regions. If a village was surrounded by sugarcane fields, say, or supported a substantial silver-mining operation, its economic livelihood dictated the type of functional elements needed, and the local craftsmen determined the distinctive styles.

An old mesquite gate guards the entrance of a ranch in Querétaro, Mexico. Courtesy Mariana Yampolsky, *La Casa Que Canta*.

One is almost always curious about the methods in which elements have been crafted or why a certain piece was created in a specific way. The universal answer? *Es la costumbre* (It is the custom). Strong traditions endure in the art of creating utilitarian and decorative elements that eventually become marked by time, memory, use, and the events of life. Methods of cooking and sleeping have changed little in centuries, and countless crafts have survived from pre-Hispanic days, among them stone and wood carving, ceramics, lacquer work, and weaving.

In addition to common furniture forms, these techniques have produced a variety of practical elements for daily use, including wooden whisks for stirring chocolate, carved *bateas* for mixing dough, cup-shaped mortars for crushing coffee beans, three-legged stools for milking goats, clay *ollas* for cooking beans, stone *molcajetes* for grinding chiles and tomatoes, hollowed-out gourds for holding tortillas, presses for making cheese, wooden plows for tilling the fields, and tree-trunk-notched ladders for accessing *tapancos*, lofts where corn is stored. On the nonpractical side, there are fine elements too: *santos*, or carved saint images; toys and masks

A collection of miniature Mexican *trasteros* hang over a brightly painted bookshelf in the Oaxacan dining room of Mr. and Mrs. Ramon Fasada. Handmade by Mr. Fasada and his son, each *trastero* is richly detailed, painted and filled with tiny clay pots.

for folk dances and ceremonies; and wooden musical instruments, from handsome guitars to primitive gourd rattles filled with clay beads and finished with fitted wood handles.

Since half of Mexico's 90 million people still live in rural locations and work the land, village life is based on a strong sense of community. A person's identity is closely tied to his family, church, and place of business, and his emotional ties to the village are strong. In this culture, the ordinary events of daily life—birth, adolescence, courtship, marriage, old age, and death—are

fully observed and commemorated. Enormous creative energy is showered onto the special objects that express the deeper meaning of these events.

Consequently, religion lies at the center of village life, a dominant and unifying force affecting many other aspects of villagers' lives. Infused with religious iconography, the color and pageantry of the fiestas and celebrations relieve the daily routines of isolated villages. No home is without a crucifix, a statue of a saint, or a religious picture. Indeed, the saints are considered part of the family and are treated with affection and familiarity.

The distinctive use of color is also an essential part of the spirit and self-expression of the Mexican people. Even the humblest homes have colorfully painted doorways and façades — personal showcases that nearly every villager manages to afford. Patios are places of expression, too, as they are typically bustling with activity, especially in the homes of small villages where the work of craftsmen — as well as much of the housekeeping — is done in an ambience inspired by fresh air, potted flowers and plants, and, not infrequently, a goat or two.

A woman amidst the daily ritual of tortilla-making. A *metate* is used to grind the corn into *masa*, and a wooden *batea* holds the dough.

Opposite: A family altar table in Coacotla, Veracruz.

Courtesy Mariana Yampolsky, *La Casa Que Canta*.

CARVED OBJECTS & VESSELS

HAND-CARVED VESSELS AND OBJECTS OF EVERY SHAPE AND DESCRIPTION ARE ABUNDANT IN Mexico, particularly in the rural markets and village centers. Embodying local family traditions, these pieces are uniquely designed to meet the specific demands of everyday life. In short, form follows function.

Giant tree trunks are carved into elongated sugar molds or cup-shaped *morteros*, or mortars, for crushing wheat and coffee beans; twisted branches are fashioned into small stools, hangers, and amusing children's toys; ox yokes, saddle forms, and *bebederos*, or feeding troughs, are designed with hearty proportions to withstand decades of weather and wear. Today these once-functional relics of daily working life have taken on new lives as cherished design accents in contemporary homes.

No two of the vessels and objects are alike, and each piece holds history in its carving. Echoing simpler times as well as the Mexican devotion to family life, work, religion, and celebrations, the objects may look commonplace in their original contexts; but once placed in contemporary settings, they become multifaceted, standing on their own as thought-provoking sculptures and furniture whose decorative details provide a pleasing reminder of Mexico's rich history and skillful craftsmen.

Originally used in an old convent, a carved mesquite press for *rebozos*, or women's shawls, now stands as sculpture under a portal.

Fitted legs support this unusual chair, shaped from a single piece of mesquite. The carved top hole allows for easy portability, whether by hand, rope, or hook.

As they appear under paintings, in gardens, behind beds, and over mantelpieces, these objects invite curiosity and tactile exploration. One is tempted to contemplate a hand-rendered shape of an ox yoke, a wooden dough bowl, or a chair carved from one solid piece of wood. The application of these elements in today's interior design allows them to add textural composition and depth to modern lives. They spark imaginations and remind of the delight of handwrought objects.

Collectors and homeowners alike have found inspiration in the diversity of these wood and stone pieces from all aspects of Mexican life, be it from the kitchen, the workshop, the farm, the ranch, the country home or the colonial building. A collection of sugar molds with round, conical indentations is newly positioned—lined up vertically at alternating heights—to create a graphically intriguing headboard in the bedroom of a New York loft. A large carved header board with pintle-hinge sockets cut into each side is reborn as a mantelpiece, its pintle holes now serving as built-in candleholders.

In an architect's home in Tucson, carved *tornillos*, or vice screw clamps on carpenters' benches, have been built into an adobe bathroom wall for use as towel racks. The natural beauty and texture of *pilas*, or stone watering troughs, have made unique sink basins in an elegant bathroom in Mexico's Lake Pátzcuaro region. Most commonly used as garden planters, these stone vessels were originally used, among other things, to water and feed livestock and to cool hot metal such as horseshoes for blacksmiths and grinding wheels made hot from sharpening tools.

Often equipped with such simple tools as axes, saws, and chisels, the craftsman reveals his ingenuity in a variety of ways. Even the simplest and most utilitarian pieces are infused with a certain wit. Some that will elicit instant smiles are simple three- or four-legged stools carved in the shapes of animals and small figures. A memorable free-form seat found in Durango resembles a man doing a one-handed push-up. Its new owner, who has given it a place of honor in his Los Angeles office, affectionately nicknamed it the "Jack Palance stool."

In addition to their decorative use in American home interiors, these common objects have also found themselves lovingly incorporated into outdoor landscapes, both in the United States and at contemporary Mexican residences. Flanking garden fountains, standing as sentinels under porticos, and nesting under stairwells, Mexican country pieces remind us of lost traditions.

This large stool carved from cypress was used for both a work surface and a seat. Apparently one leg got too close to the fire, as evidenced by its charred tip.

A mesquite *quesero*, or cheese press, from central Mexico has been amusingly carved into the shape of a pig. Its function is additionally amusing as the channel leading from the hole in the pig's head to its mouth allows for excess water drainage. Today its posture is one of welcome; it stands at the entrance of a formal dining room. Collection of Omer and Bunny Claiborne.

A special affinity for culinary antiques such as wooden tortilla presses, ladles, and grain-measure boxes—the unusual and utilitarian—often leads to searches in remote locations high in the mountains of southern Mexico. On one such trip, an hour-long burro ride was endured to reach a dormant coffee plantation where large coffee *morteros* and *manos,* or large pounding sticks carved from durable hardwoods, were discovered. Though coffee hadn't been crushed in the mortars for several years, the aroma of the beans was still pungent. Even after the three-foot-tall vessels were shipped back to the United States, they were redolent of Oaxacan *cafe.*

Above: Originally used for crushing coffee beans and wheat, Mexican *morteros,* or mortars, are hand carved from massive tree trunks. Very often, the wood's natural shapes are worked into the design, allowing for natural handholds—gnarled knots in the wood add sculptural depth—as seen here in the *mortero's* handle.

Right: A mesquite *bebedero,* or feeding trough, has been patched with a thin strip of tin.

Opposite: An old sugar mold, or *molde de azucar,* features conical-shaped indentations for making brown sugar. Collection of Karen Witynski and Joe Carr.

Homegrown chiles and spices are essential to the Mexican diet, which means that the following elements are present in every Mexican kitchen: *metates*, or grinding stones; *molcajetes*, or small stone mortars used especially for grinding spices; and wooden *bateas*, or dough bowls. Side by side, they play a vital role in the daily ritual of tortilla-making and sauce preparation. Found in a variety of shapes, the most common *batea* is rectangular with rounded edges and has a depth of approximately three to six inches. Larger sizes can be found in restaurants and *panaderias*, or bakeries, where greater quantities of ingredients are used; and even larger, more robust *bateas* were carved from thicker pieces of wood and used for such hearty tasks as washing clothes or soaking craft materials such as *amate*, or bark paper.

A familiar sight in American homes and retail shops from Connecticut to Seattle, *bateas* have become one of the most popular modern design accessories. As multipurpose containers, they have adapted to hold apples, garden tools, or bath soaps, and have shown off treasured collections of beach glass and crystal doorknobs. In Banana Republic stores, they are equally at home displaying colorful sweaters and other accessories.

Other essentials of daily Mexican life are small worktables and stools. Hearty, functional pieces carved from single blocks of wood, their versatility is proved throughout the home and workplace. The most universal shape—a round disc with fitted legs—is commonly referred to as an *escabel*, or milking stool. These all-purpose seats are usually carved symmetrically with smooth surfaces; others make use of thicker wood specimens. Some styles include carved handles on one side for easy transportation. Low, round tortilla tables are recognizable in this way by a small, carved handhold area extending horizontally from the surface.

Although Mexican *carpinteros* first and foremost had to be skilled traditional furniture makers, many of them also carved altar screens, angels, and saints for the local churches and village residents. Many were also

commissioned to craft special patron saints and crosses for home altars and annual ceremonies and fiestas.

Country vessels and objects often date back several centuries—indeed, the *molcajete* is well documented as stemming from the pre-Columbian era—and yet its presence today in our homes, offices, gardens, and stores adds warmth and texture to even the most modern spaces. Radiant with the personal touch of individual hands, these pieces have attracted many new admirers. Their new, extended lives make it possible for their artistry to touch many generations to come.

Above: A *batea* becomes the perfect vessel to display sweaters in a Banana Republic store.

Right: A coffee mortar is filled with gourds to mimic the shapes of an African sausage tree's fruit.

Opposite: A *batea*, or dough bowl, finds a new decorative use next to a contemporary painting by Mara Beth Witynski.

26

DOORS & ENTRANCEWAYS

BY NATURE EVERY DOOR IS A MYSTERY, HINTING AT WHAT LIES BEHIND, AND IN MEXICO, THE lives behind the doors are as varied and intriguing as the doors themselves. A casual stroll through the twisting streets and tiled sidewalks of Mexico's provincial towns yields strong impressions, and around the entranceways, one can see life in full stride. Locals regularly assemble before the *puertas* of pink or yellow sandstone churches; quiet gossip is exchanged on the *zócalos*, or public squares, in the shade of centuries-old cypress trees, and in the doorways of *panaderías*, or bakeries, or in the hotels. Street vendors rest on the stone steps of private homes, while giggling schoolchildren and pets roam past the backdrops of textured walls. The sheer variety of doors and entrances keeping quiet company on a single street is amazing. Whether they are weathered or newly repaired, one can learn a great deal about the detail and design of old shutters, doors, gates, and window guards. One can also get a colorful peek at daily Mexican life because the doors are often left open.

Pasé, pasé is the quickly spoken phrase heard all over Mexico when one is waved and welcomed through an entrance. More often than not, when antique buyers have been invited inside someone's home or place of business, they find themselves lingering longer in the entranceway, hoping to ogle the door for a few more seconds, trying to soak up all of its detail—whether it's

An intriguing hallway lined with old weathered Mexican doors and shutters leads to the restoration workshop of José Martinez.

a heart-shaped lock plate, or an unusual iron latch sporting a lizard head, or simply someone's initials carved into a panel. So as not to appear rude or hesitant about a host's invitation, buyer's try to stifle this tendency, or at least signal to another buyer to follow the host immediately, allowing one to dawdle a little longer.

When one considers how many old doors are still in use in Mexico, one's next thought might be how well they must have been made to survive the many years of use and weathering. A tribute to their skilled craftsmen, exterior doors were made from the most durable hardwoods, including mesquite and *sabino*, which are favored for their extreme density and natural resistance to insect infestation.

There is no end to the style and variety of doors seen in Mexico. The only constant is that most doors come in pairs, the planks held together by iron braces and large round-headed *clavos*, or hand-forged nails. The larger the door, the heavier and thicker the wood used. The massive doors of haciendas, churches, and government buildings required oversized *clavos*, often three to four inches in diameter, their decorative heads filled with brass. These larger *chapetons* were often shaped into stars or ornate designs. The grandest in scale, *zaguán* entrance doors still exist in the old colonial towns. They radiate a compelling sense of history, for they were built large enough to admit wagons into a home's inner courtyard and usually had smaller doors set within the larger ones, allowing pedestrians to enter without opening the larger pair.

Arched raised-panel *alacena*, or built-in cabinet, from Santa Maria del Oro, Durango. Collection of Jack and Peggy Calderella.

Opposite: A weathered pair of mesquite doors lead to an inner courtyard through an adobe wall. Home of Ron and Suzie Dubin, Santa Fe, New Mexico.

More common colonial styles feature pairs of doors with intricate raised-panel designs reminiscent of old Spain, while others can be as plain and simple as hand-adzed flat panels set inside a wooden frame. These single-panel doors are also referred to as *hojas*, which actually means panel. Double doors then become *dos hojas*, and Dutch doors *quatro hojas*. In the rural areas, there are many beautiful yet simple styles dictated by the lack of sophisticated tools. As the homes in most villages and towns were built close together for security, the colors, textures, and details of their doors can be viewed directly from the sidewalk. From walking a single block, one can experience centuries of wear, old braces, native repairs, and heavily adzed surfaces. A person can also detect the locations of original old wood doors, long since replaced by metal pairs, by looking above the tops of doors at the surviving pediments of wooden spindles or splats that were made to match the original doors.

The various designs range from raw unadorned wood to raised rectangular panels, raised diamond patterns, vertical designs, grooved-panel outlines, and fluted doors, or *puertas de raya* patterns. On some, important occasions, *dichos* (pertinent sayings), or names of respected or noteworthy family members are carved into lintels above the front door. More detailed styles feature an open-window section on top, inset with vertical iron bars or lathe-turned wooden spindles. Some have small openings on the bottom end of the door with small semicircle cutouts for family cats or dogs. *Rejas*, or wrought-iron grilles, cover many of the street-facing windows of elaborate *casas* and government buildings in larger towns, while even the simplest buildings are protected by horizontal bars of *otote*, bamboo, or wooden spindles set into the adobe walls.

Single doors are not as widely seen and are mostly found in rural homes and storage buildings or barns. These single *hojas* are uniformly around five feet in height and, since they don't meet American building

codes, they are the first doors to make the transition to become coffee tables or built-in doors for cabinets or entertainment units. Most of these single flat-panel styles were designed with wooden pintle hinges, as they were the easiest to make in the countryside where iron was either unavailable or unaffordable. Not as strong as iron—though certainly durable for a long time if made from hardwoods—the pintle is actually part of the door, carved and protruding from the same wood, and extends to fit into holes specially fashioned into the door frame so that the door swings on them and

Iron *corchetes* (hook-and-eye latches) used here to lock a pair of mesquite doors from the inside (left), and a pair of *postigos*, or inner shutters, (right).

does not need metal hinges. Certainly, after a lot of use, the wooden pintles break off; many today are found in that state.

In addition to a variety of *chapas*, or iron lock plates, on the front doors, the reverse sides feature *corchetes*, or hook-and-eye latches, so that, upon entry, one can lock oneself in, or sometimes latch an iron crossbar into place.

Ample walls secure the secrets of many old villages and towns, as homes are built right to the sidewalk. Massive, bleak exteriors are brightened by bold doors in rich blues, reds, and greens, some with remnants of old color and others freshly repainted. In many of the older sections

34

of town, eighteenth-century-style doors with massive *clavos* and decorative bosses can still be seen on churches. Two of our favorites include the bright blue majesty of La Iglesia de Santa Monica in Guadalajara, and La Basilica de Zapopan. In sharp contrast to the simpler country styles, these are wonderful large-scale colonial specimens; one can only imagine the extensive work involved to enable them to withstand the punishments of time. They are remarkable testaments to the craftsmen and the indigenous hardwoods used, and a good reference point for comparing woods.

In the coastal towns and villages, doors take on a different character, representative of the local materials and the climate, which calls for fresh breezes as ventilation. From the *palapas*, or palm-thatched structures, of Yalapa to the simple forms in Oaxaca, doors are sometimes made by thatching together palm fronds or assembling wide bamboo pieces and tying them with natural fibers. Occasionally there are no doors at all, as is the case with some open-air *palapas*. When wooden doors are used in these regions, they are usually louvered or are pairs that feature *postigos*, or hinged shutters within the larger doors, that open easily to admit air or light. These inner shutters are also called *ventanitas*, or little windows, and are cut in diverse shapes with intricate iron latches on the inside.

Veracruz and Acapulco overflow with these ancient, peekaboo-style doors hinting at life inside. While walking early in the morning in Acapulco's old section of town, we have often witnessed street vendors with their baskets of freshly baked sweet breads passing plump *tortas* and tortillas through such *postigos*, enabling the lady of the house to keep her children safely inside. The same style doors are seen throughout interior Mexico as well. Not only do they lend themselves to casual conversation among passersby, but they provide a natural meeting place for courting *novios*, or young lovers, who want to sneak a quick *beso*, or kiss.

In the ranch areas of Durango, Sonora, and San Luis Potosí, Dutch doors are used prolifically in confining animals while allowing cross breezes. On the barn doors and outbuildings of these regions, it is common to see brands burned into the planks. Some antique buyers have also discovered very old, faint drawings on the inside of these rustic doors — usually a figure of some sort. One favorite was the comical face of a man in a sombrero. Perhaps a few creative ranch hands sought levity in a spare moment by lending their artistic talents to the inside of this door. Corral gates were usually fashioned from long horizontal planks and were always made of mesquite, one of the strongest woods for heavy use.

On the subject of durability and security, the *puerta de carcel*, or jail door, is another prevalent type in Mexico. Almost always made of mesquite and often reinforced on the outside with iron straps running across the latticework design, these doors are as strong as they come. Most examples have been found with charred burn marks on the bottom where prisoners probably attempted escape by trying to burn down the door. As mesquite is one of the densest woods, it would take a bonfire-size blaze to destroy it.

In the commercial sections of town, busy wall-art images advertising the services of each establishment vie with multicolored, flowery patios partially concealed by spindled gates. New iron security doors guard some shops, yet many retain their original wood styles, sometimes with a panel or two having been replaced. Wrought iron is seen in a variety of styles from practical and basic to more ornate, depending on which section of town one is in. Children play on the tile sidewalks or narrow cement paths. Though underfoot, they never seem to be in the way, their resonant, cheerful laughter competing with church bells and the whistles and calls of street vendors peddling their fresh *churros* or *refrescos*. Framing these street-gallery scenes are the truly intriguing doors and entrances of the houses and courtyards.

A *gozne* hinge detail.

Young friends make use of a Guadalajara door's *postigo* for easy conversation.

Opposite: A pair of pine doors from Michoacán feature a *postigo*, or inner shutter, on one side. Home of Jerry and Carolyn Reichow.

With the addition of strong hinges and hardware, it is easy to understand why many Mexican doors are still in such hearty condition. Excellent carpentry work was used to assemble them and special care was taken with the iron hardware, as Mexicans have excelled at ironwork for centuries. Early door styles feature snipe or eyelet hinges, commonly referred to as *gozne* hinges. Easily recognizable, they were one of the more prominent styles used during the colonial period and through the late 1800s. Composed of two wrought-iron elements resembling interlocking cotter pins, each piece consists of an eye and two flat parallel spikes that taper to a point. One piece is mounted on the door at the corner, its spikes driven into the wood or inserted into a predrilled hole at a 45-degree angle. The points that emerge on the opposite side of the wood are spread and clinched. The other piece is installed in the door jamb, also at a 45-degree angle. When in place, the interlocking eyes of the hinge are at right corners to each other and thus move freely when the door opens or closes.

In addition to the myriad styles of doors and entrances, there are just as many color combinations. Some of the most unlikely somehow always work in the context of their relationship to the street as a whole. Window shutters were constructed in much the same way as the larger doors, only smaller and often featuring four symmetrical panels. The favored colors for them seem to be blue, red, and green though we have seen some that were crafted for interior *alacenas*, or cupboards, built into kitchen walls that were left natural while one pair was painted pink.

In the towns touched more by the modern age, boldly painted facades are seen in continually contrasting patterns of color and tile juxtaposed with wainscoting. Perhaps mixing and clashing with a neighbor's blue-and-white horizontal theme might be someone else's green-and-yellow stripes. These more modern streets are really fun to see, as some contrasts are so harsh and unexpected that they actually work from a graphic art perspective.

"THE MEXICAN DOORS WE USE IN OUR DESIGN WORK GIVE SOUL, CHARACTER AND SHAPE TO OUR HOUSES. I LOVE THE BEAUTY OF THEIR 'LIVED-IN-NESS' AND ESPECIALLY LOVE THE TEXTURES OF THE HAND-PLANED PIECES THAT SIMPLY FEEL GOOD! LIKE THEIR MAKERS, THESE DOORS CARRY NO PRETENSE, AND HELP CONNECT ME TO A HISTORY AND A PEOPLE THAT I REALLY TREASURE."
—KAREN VAUGHAN
INTERIOR DESIGNER

A popular movement in the past twenty years has been toward single wrought-iron front doors with heavy, lathed, expanded iron screens or backings, which allow breezes to pass through but not animals or insects. This has resulted in many sets of old wooden doors being put on the market for sale.

In today's contemporary design contexts, weathered Mexican doors are being restored and adapted to a variety of architectural settings. They make the transition to doors on entertainment units, closets, and master bedrooms, and are designed into headboards and coffee tables as their simplicity and time-honored presence complement many interior design styles.

A guest-house entrance features a pair of doors designed with *quatro hojas*, or four panels, to allow for fresh breezes and sunlight.

Opposite: A 200-year-old mesquite door rests horizontally now, easily transformed into a contemporary dining table flanked by leather cab chairs. Collection of Karen Witynski and Joe Carr.

TABLES

THE MEXICAN TABLE IS CHERISHED FOR WHAT IT REPRESENTS—A WARM HEARTH, SUSTAINING food, a sense of nurturing and nourishment that goes far beyond the kitchen. The focal point of every home, *mesas*, or tables, provide the quintessential gathering place for family meals. More than any other piece of furniture, the table is the most versatile in Mexican life, moving easily between the home and workplace, markets and celebrations. Some are grand, some are modest, but they all share in the spirit of a distinct land and hold an important place in nearly all activities. Not only are interesting tables found in the *mercado*, or marketplace, but they are present throughout the workshops and dwellings of ranches, coastal villages, and the colonial towns of present-day Mexico. Even the most humble home, if it has nothing else, usually has one table. Whatever its size, it is the focus of family life and is considered the most essential piece of furniture.

Since colonial times, display tables, *mesas de carniceros*, or butcher tables, and even altar tables have kept company together at the local *mercado*. Certainly one of the easiest places to see the tremendous range of shapes and sizes, the *mercado* contains a smorgasbord of design styles. The most prolific are the simple dining tables and benches found at market-stall restaurants. These handcrafted pieces feature mortise-and-tenon construction and often beautiful legs— turned, painted, tapered, or carved—each kind with its own subtle design characteristics.

A five-foot diameter table with elaborate cutout legs holds court in a dining room surrounded by contemporary chairs and accents.

Above: Pine corner tables, or *rinconeras*, of this style were extremely popular in the latter part of the nineteenth century. This example is from Aguascalientes, Mexico. Collection of Galeria San Ysidro.

Below: This popular ranch-style table features splayed legs and cross stretchers. Its mesquite top shows years of use, and a pine base reveals original red paint.

Opposite: A mesquite ranch table displays a collection of candleholders in the contemporary kitchen of Morton and Donna Fleischer's MorDō Ranch in Scottsdale, Arizona.

Visits to the marketplace have revealed tapered-leg tables from Durango displaying onions and radishes, shorter painted tables holding old scales for weighing almonds, and bakeries in which once-sharp counter-front corners and molding detail have been softened over time by decades of people brushing against their sides.

Regional styles are distinct—tables from the colonial town of Queré-taro feature conservatively turned legs, whereas those of coastal farming towns in Guerrero have simple squared legs with stretchers. Even in more decorative forms, the beautiful chip-carved pine of Michoacán is distinguished from the Victorian-inspired turned legs and apron cutouts of northern Chihuahua.

In one day's walk through a provincial town in the state of Oaxaca, many contexts are discovered in which Mexican tables support aspects of this culture's work and religious life. In the state of Oaxaca, the town's public letter writer is seated at a painted, turned-leg yellow table, its vivid color announcing his presence. In the side room of an adjacent church, a long, six-legged rectangular table supports a handful of revered patron saints. Auto-shop workers down the street are repairing a broken carburetor on a robust mesquite ranch table cut in thick proportions expressly to sustain the kind of abuse it bears. On the outskirts of town, a candle factory prepares its product for packing atop a thin pine table with octagonal legs. Two drawers on either side contain precut wax sheets for individual candle wrapping. Food preparation in a restaurant is accomplished on a large single-slab table with A-frame legs, found this day covered with serrano chiles and carrots on their way to becoming soup. A tailor's shop features a taller, thirty-four-inch table with convenient large drawers for pins and threads. Underneath, the bottom stretchers around the base cross in an "X" motif.

Above: A simple ranch-style table is in use at a Jalisco market.

Right: A *mesa de carnicero*, or butcher's table, displays fresh chicken at a Oaxacan market.

Opposite: A large butcher's table from Puebla has found another use in the Oaxacan kitchen of Rene Bustamente and Ann Miller.

Observation of thousands of tables over a number of years has led to distinguishing certain styles that are associated with particular areas. Although there are exceptions to all rules, some styles stand out and are the most familiar.

Tables from the regions surrounding the state of Zacatecas are made predominately from local heart pine called *corazón de yarín*. A large percentage have gracefully turned legs, and the aprons and legs are painted with bright colors—mostly blues, greens, and yellows. One revealing characteristic of this region is the placement of small cutout braces in the upper corners where the apron meets the leg.

Traveling south around the shores of Lake Pátzcuaro in the state of Michoacán, one notices tables made exclusively from pine, and the legs are also delicately turned. Practiced in seventeenth-century Spain, chip- or gouge-carving is a method of embellishing wood that has flourished in this state for centuries. Native Tarascan Indians of this region excelled in the art, using the technique to ornament chairs, table aprons, and *trasteros*.

The predominant table design throughout central and western Mexico is referred to among dealers and buyers as "ranch-style," or *"mesa ranchero*." These pieces feature square-legs, A-frame construction, and end stretchers that are higher than those at the side. The mortised stretchers, or *largeros*, sometimes join the legs to create a box-like enclosure. This particular style can be altered to become a functional desk with ample leg room by simply removing the front stretcher.

These ranch-style tables are predominantly made from mesquite or *sabino*—often a combination of the two. Close to the coastal areas of Colima and Guerrero, Spanish cedar and *parota* are the woods of choice. Although there are additional styles, such as the Mennonite tables from Chihuahua and the Victorian-influenced pieces from San Luis Potosí, they are not as widely seen compared with the above three examples.

The real heart of the house is the kitchen, and its table is the center of the activity. The *mesa de cocina*, or kitchen table, not only serves as the gathering place for meals and celebrations among relatives but also for important family decisions. *Tocineras*, or pork tables, with their deep-drawer construction, are used in some kitchens for food preparation and meat

Opposite: Painted pine kitchen table from Durango is massive in size with large stocky legs. Handmade molding outlines both drawers. Leg features a handy Coca-Cola bottle opener affixed to its side. El Paso Imports Collection.

Below: An early example of a Zacatecas table shows the cutout corner brace. Handmade molding outlines drawer. El Paso Imports Collection.

49

A Zacatecas dining table with painted Mexican chairs complements the mood of this serene dining room. Collection of Virginia Dwan.

Opposite: An old *sabino* ranch table glows with a butterscotch patina in the center of a grand living room that opens to a colonial courtyard. A turn-of-the-century Mexican ceramic pot and glass paperweight add a touch of contemporary color. Collection of Ed Holler and Sam Saunders.

drying. Drawers on other tables make them useful as sideboards, and sometimes lower worktables are used in both the kitchen and outdoors to assist in crafts-making duties and other preparations such as soaking hibiscus petals for making refreshing drinks. *Rinconeras* are corner tables used in either living rooms or bedrooms, and a *mesa de centro* is a table used in the center of the home or dining room.

Inside most every Mexican home, the altar display, usually staged on a table or a shelf, serves as a sort of mecca for family keepsakes and religious items. Lovingly assembled atop a *mesa de altar*, or altar table, are candles, containers of fresh or paper flowers, carved-wooden *santos*, various hand-made crosses, family photos of loved ones, or even favorite pet pictures.

Found in butcher shops and at the marketplace, *mesas de carniceros* are constructed of hearty proportions to withstand the chopping of butcher's knives and cleavers. Two vertical beams rising from the side of the table support a horizontal beam with iron hooks from which fresh meats can be hung. These tables make ideal prep tables, the iron hooks useful for hanging anything from heads of garlic to pots and pans. No use is ruled out—vanilla candles were seen draped from such hooks in a *mercado* adjacent to the local *iglesia*, or church.

While driving through Puebla, one collector stopped for lunch and struck up a conversation with a butcher working at his *mesa de carnicero*, which was entirely covered with freshly chopped meat. Although the table's thick mesquite legs were all that were visible, the collector admired the robust proportions and age of the table and told the butcher he would love to buy it for his home, though he realized it was a vital workpiece for the butcher. The butcher then revealed that he would soon be moving to Mexico City to retire and didn't need to keep the table; he was happy to sell it. After washing away the residues, the table top revealed decades of chop-mark patterns and large handwrought nails.

STORAGE
& SEATING

No home would be complete without the numerous cupboards, shelves, closets, boxes, and other nooks and crannies for storing personal items that help to maintain order in living spaces. In themselves, storage elements account for some of the most diverse antiques found in Mexico.

Every culture has a distinct style by which it is identified. In Mexico, however, a country with many different cultures, a variety of factors contribute to the design and style of Mexican storage furniture. Many of these elements were brought to the New World from Europe during the colonial period, while others evolved over time out of local cultures.

As in Spain, the chest was the single most important item of furniture in early Mexico. Certainly the most common, boxes, chests, and trunks served multiple purposes as safeguards for valuables, storage for food and clothing, support boards for dining or sleeping, and surfaces for writing. These containers were made of many different materials and were decorated both simply and elaborately. The most common woods used for trunks were and continue to be Spanish cedar; *sabino*, or Mexican cypress; and mesquite. *Petacas*, or leather traveling trunks of Spanish origin, are among the earliest colonial examples and are well represented in history books and museums.

An old cedar trunk focuses the eye on folk carvings and artifacts in the entrance hall of Rene Bustamente and Ann Miller's home.

Morton and Donna Fleischer of Scottsdale, Arizona, have added Mexican country pieces to their MorDō Ranch. Their extensive Western Memorabilia Collection includes saddles, holsters, spurs, bits, and chaps. Amid their display is an old *dispensario*, or trunk, used for dispensing grains.

Below: Spanish cedar and cypress provided the raw wood for these old trunks at the Joshua Baer Gallery.

In colonial times, large *arcónes*, or wide chests, were used in churches and convents to store vestments and chalices as well as sacred documents. Many *arcónes* featured feet at the corners; detailed *chapas*, or lock plates; and iron strips used for joint reinforcement. Storage chests for household use, in contrast, were very plain, their surface decoration usually consisting of no more than simple dovetailing or decorative paint. Two styles found inside the home include *petaquillas*, or small trunks, used for clothing storage—often with iron handles attached for easy transportation—and *baúles*, similar to *petaquillas*, only not easily transportable. Considered a much more permanent fixture in the house, *baúles* did not usually have handles. Very often they featured rounded or domed tops and had matching bases with simple turned legs. These styles are contemporarily converted into side tables by cutting the tops down to create flat surfaces.

One of the most common pieces of furniture found throughout all the states of Mexico, the storage chest is a treasured piece in the home. Inside, each bears the personal signature of its owner(s). Interior lids are usually lined with decorative paper—sometimes floral prints or a montage of paper prayer cards—and sprinkled with small photographs of family members and paintings of patron saints. Almost always included is a picture of Jesus or Our Lady of Guadalupe amidst the other mementos and paper clippings.

Another type of trunk is the *dispensario*, or grain chest, used for storing and dispensing dry foods such as beans, rice, and corn. Long and narrow, the *dispensario* often has several convenient compartments for food storage, and is raised off the ground to deter rodents. Dovetailed grain-measure boxes are a needed accessory used in conjunction with these trunks and have a variety of other market uses as well. Lending warmth to working and living environments, Mexican trunks have become highly prized additions to American personal spaces. Native American art dealer Joshua Baer

A unique organ-cactus motif decorates the skirt and crest of this intricately carved colonial armoire, now a cool dark storehouse encasing fine wines in the home of Jane Fonda and Ted Turner.

chose to incorporate a collection of Mexican trunks into the design of his contemporary Santa Fe gallery. He said, "I was attracted by their rich patinas and worn edges that instantly softened the precise lines of my newly finished space. The trunks reflected the feeling of age and quality that I wanted for presenting and displaying my Navajo blankets and artifacts."

Tall, freestanding cabinets popularly known as *trasteros* are primarily used in kitchens for storing dishes and food. Top shelves are either open or

A contemporary steel base has given functional height to an old cypress *arcón*.

covered by spindled or slatted doors. Bottom shelves often have round indentations for easy placement of water jars. The top of the *trastero* customarily features a decorative crest around the cornice, often in a wavy, scallop design or repeating pattern. Heavily used, *trasteros* are sometimes uniquely personalized with unusual shelf linings. One memorable *trastero's* shelves were efficiently lined with old, green coffee-can labels, echoing the green color of its painted exterior.

The design of a woven *petate*, or sleeping mat, has been carved into the surface of this 1920s cypress *trastero* from Celaya, Guanajuato. Collection of Ed Holler and Sam Saunders.

This brightly painted pine *ropero* features bouquets of flowers on each door and each side panel, accenting the cornice of this cabinet, which is reminiscent of designs on Asian furniture. El Paso Imports Collection.

Armarios are used both in homes and businesses to store valuables, important records, ledgers, and sometimes clothing. These enormous cabinets are crafted with built-in drawers and carved or raised-panel, full-length doors. They also feature large locks to secure the doors. Many early *armarios* were painted with decorative floral designs, religious icons, or city scenes, and were usually the most important and valuable pieces of furniture in the home. As they were expensive, *armarios* were out of reach of many Mexican families and only found in the wealthiest households.

The *ropero*, a tall cabinet with full-length doors in which clothing is usually stored, derives its name from the word *ropa*, meaning clothing. *Roperos* were essentially early closets, offering a choice of storage as items could either be hung on rods or folded and stacked on inside shelves. Some examples feature two drawers built inside the cabinet at the bottom for protective storage. Most *roperos* are very simple and are usually painted on the outside. Many examples have also been found with brightly colored paint or decorative paper lining the interior.

Two kinds of wooden wall shelves—*repisas* and *alacenas*—are found in Mexican homes. The *repisa*, a wall-hanging single or double shelf, is used in many ways. First and foremost, it is used for storing dry spices and sweets in the kitchen. It is also used in other rooms as a convenient shelf on which to place cherished keepsakes and photographs. Sometimes *repisas* are hung over altar tables to hold candles and religious paintings.

Larger than *repisas*, *alacenas* are cupboards that are built into walls and covered with shutters. They have shelves on the inside and are useful in rooms in which there is limited floor space. The doors range from simple raised panels to complex spindles or slats, and are sometimes chip-carved.

Comedors, or sideboards, whether simple or ornate, were most commonly seen in haciendas and wealthy colonial homes. More modest households used tables as sideboards, with members serving themselves and then sitting in chairs and eating from a plate on their laps. Even today sideboards from the colonial era and late 1800s are rare and difficult to find. The exception is in Chihuahua where very simple styles were produced in abundance. A popular piece in dining rooms today, the sideboard is a functional, sought-after item. The contemporary market has responded to the demand for sideboards by crafting styles that offer ample storage and beautifully carved raised panels of reclaimed wood.

A magnificent example of a spindled pine *armario* from Zacatecas. El Paso Imports Collection.

SEATING

Like habanero chiles are to the Mexican diet, the ladder-backed, rush-seated cantina chair—so named for its widespread use in restaurants—is a staple of the Mexican kitchen. This chair is the answer to the often-asked question: "What kind of Mexican chairs will work with my table?" Simple and sturdy cantina chairs are colorfully painted with flower and bird motifs, and feature open mortise-and-tenon construction.

Offering a bit more comfort at the table, the ubiquitous *equipales*, or indigenous high-backed barrel-shaped chairs, feature pigskin leather

stretched over a framework of bentwood, joined with glued pitch pine and secured with a cedar-slat base. *Equipale* chairs and tables are favored for their indoor/outdoor versatility and their time-enhanced patina, growing increasingly lustrous with wear.

Around coffee tables and in courtyard or patio settings, the classic Mexican *butaca*, or sling-back chair, is favored for its graceful lines and elegant comfort. The leg design and construction dates to techniques used in sixteenth-century New Spain. The seat is customarily made of leather; however, in Veracruz, it is made with cane for coolness, and in

Above: This pine chair with spindled back comes from Chihuahua. El Paso Imports Collection.

Above left: Colonial-style cypress bench features intricate cutout on top of the backboard. El Paso Imports Collection.

Opposite: An old cypress *armario* with raised panels is surrounded by a grouping of early Mexican chairs and stools in the living room of Omer and Bunny Claiborne.

Tehuantepec, wooden cross slats form the back and seat. Today its classic style persists, though its popularity has spawned a variety of contemporary interpretations.

In addition to the above-mentioned examples, many other chair styles are found in Mexico, including the straight-backed side chairs with chip-carving designs, wooden-barrel armchairs, and the *sillón de frailero*, or friar's chair, influenced from the styles in sixteenth-century Spain. In very rural areas, small children's chairs feature seats woven of jute or rawhide thongs, often interwoven with wider strips of tire tread.

Gathering to gossip in the shade of centuries-old trees or to rest on benches as the parade of daily life idles by is a favorite pastime in Mexico. *Bancos*, or benches, are most visible in the courtyards of municipal buildings, around the shaded *zócalos*, and under the portals of plazas. One can encounter the inherent friendliness of the Mexican people simply by sitting on a bench anywhere in Mexico. Old men will inquire where a newcomer is from, children will quizzically ask about the person's shoes, and candy vendors will tempt him with their sweets. The full view of Mexican life is entirely accessible from a languid shady bench.

Long *bancos* were first used in the refectories of old monasteries and public buildings. Small benches and stools are most prevalent at the marketplace and in the work areas of homes and shops. They are always close by, available for enjoying a meal or for sitting and visiting with a vendor or even for getting one's shoes shined. From the most simply crafted three-legged *escabeles*, or milking stools, carved from single pieces of wood, to the free-form shapes that have evolved from gnarled tree knots, small Mexican benches and stools take on countless shapes and forms.

Below: A pair of *butacas* made in the workshop of William Spratling, circa 1940. His signature brand appears stamped on the back. Only Yesterday, Miami, Florida.

Opposite above: A blue Zacatecas scalloped bench with coffee mortar and water filter stand are well suited for this New Mexico portal. Collection of Ron and Suzie Dubin. Design by Susan Dupépé.

Opposite below: A hearty mesquite bench from Durango features a cutout design and sits comfortably on a patio at the Matteucci residence in Santa Fe, New Mexico.

MEXICAN INFLUENCES

CELEBRATED FOR THEIR SIMPLE SPLENDOR, THE ANTIQUES OF OLD MEXICO HAVE TAKEN UP residence in innovative interiors, gardens, and commercial settings on both sides of the border. Embraced by designers and homeowners alike, Mexico's relics of real life are pure and practical, beautiful yet unpretentious. This versatility has allowed them to integrate easily into a variety of architectural environments. On a tropical-island retreat, in a minimalist New York loft, or inside an Austin ranch in the hill country, the furniture and architectural objects of Mexico complement a variety of design styles.

To design and furnish a space using country pieces opens the door to remarkable possibility and endless invention. Doors are now more than doors. They have new extended lives as dining tables, headboards, and decorative art. Window lintels become handsome mantel pieces, and old balcony balustrades serve as table bases.

In the Montana ranch home of Ted Turner and Jane Fonda, a welcoming front entrance unites a pair of Mexican doors into an impressive single door. Permanently impressed on the panel is a cattle brand of the letter "T," on the other "J." Interestingly, the engraved letters were not custom-branded for the owners. They were, like the doors themselves, "found" as they are in Mexico. Upon the serendipitous discovery, their designer quickly worked them into the project.

A Oaxacan table displays Mexican ceramics and colonial candlesticks on a colorful portal. Home of Ed Holler and Sam Saunders.

Additionally, an old Mexican tailor's table serves as a dining-room buffet, its original green paint enhancing the warmth of the room's wood floors and nearby stone fireplace. A unique organ-cactus motif decorates the skirt and crest of their intricately carved colonial armoire, now a cool, dark store-house encasing their fine wines.

Opposite: An old tailor's table now serves as a dining buffet.

The welcoming front entrance of Jane Fonda and Ted Turner's Montana ranch house unites a pair of Mexican doors into an impressive single door.

Since moving to the Southwest from New York, artist and collector James Havard has had an enthusiastic eye for Mexican country pieces, especially carved mortars, painted trunks on stands, and tables that

Seen from the back, these mesquite doors with remnants of old paint have been cleverly joined in the center to make one solid entrance door. Collection of James Havard.

Opposite: An intricately designed apron on this pine table from Zacatecas is the center of attention amongst a grouping of eclectic treasures. Painting by James Havard.

combine paint and detail for a colorful presence. His house has become a compelling showcase for contemporary art, Mexican furniture and architectural antiques, Native American art, and American folk art. His

A pair of mesquite doors open from the study loft to a balcony above a living room lined with Mexican dance masks. Home of Rene Bustamente and Ann Miller.

Opposite: A Chihuahua pine bed, Day of the Dead masks, and ethnic jewelry strike an eclectic theme in the guest room of Rene Bustamente and Ann Miller.

painted-blue entrance door alerts visitors that they are in for a visual experience both inside and out. A dedicated gardener, Havard has preserved and dried his crop of roses and wildflowers for display in old mesquite *morteros*, colorful milk cans, and primitive pottery, all bursting with the spirit of his garden. The divine highlight of his home—his hillside garden—is crowned by an adobe building designed as a small chapel that opens up with large Mexican doors to reveal a potting shed complete with tool storage, Mexican trunks, and a *trastero*, a true heaven-on-earth location.

The warm, rich hardwoods of Mexican grain *morteros* play subtly with a pair of sculptural African stepladders and textures in a painting by Lynne Gelfman.

Opposite below: The Gelfman's neon hallway is dramatized by the presence of a Mexican coffee *mortero* and masks.

High on a hill overlooking the pre-Columbian Zapotec capital of Monte Albán and the old colonial city of Oaxaca sits the elegant, open-air home of Rene Bustamente and artist Ann Miller. Together they have designed, built, and decorated an inviting contemporary home, filled with relics of celebration and worship. As a research anthropologist, Bustamente has spent many years traveling to remote villages, researching the customs

and ceremonies of Mexican celebrations. Their extensive collection of Mexican dance masks is a vibrant mosaic upon the colored walls and stairwells of their home.

Their light-filled bedroom is softened by avocado green walls and features an adaptation of an old Chihuahua ranch bed with a mosquito-net canopy. A pair of old Mexican doors lead to the large kitchen, which

opens onto a breezy portal running the length of the house. A butcher's table is the kitchen's focal point, its thick splayed legs and exposed iron *clavos* testifying to its solidity as a work surface. Hung right in the center of their upstairs loft-like library, a colorful hammock provides an ideal getaway space for reading or dozing. No desks and chairs are needed here.

Contemporary painter Lynne Gelfman is passionate about texture, which is evident in her rich abstract paintings and her collection of Latin

Coffee *morteros* hold court beneath flowering angel trumpet blossoms in the tropical garden of Jacques and Claudia Auger, Hibiscus Island, Florida.

American textiles, baskets, and Mexican country elements. She and her husband, Dan, favor pieces that possess rich patinas and wear marks, hinting at their previous utilitarian lives. Their coffee mortar is filled with silver balls from China and sits at the entrance of their neon-striped hallway that opens to their light-filled studio. Outside surrounding the pool are exotic banana trees, a collection of volcanic stone mortars and pestles brought back from their travels, and another *mortero*, this time holding towels for

Color livens up this airy courtyard and stairwell in the Morelia home of Dr. and Mrs. Alfredo Sosa Rojas. *Bateas* sit atop the stairs with planted herbs.

swimmers. Equally passionate about Mexican accents, the Gelfmans collect charming ex-voto paintings and objects that are graced with the Lady of Guadalupe image—from car accessories to naive drawings. Even their modern kitchen is sparked with the colors of today's Mexican market—pink and yellow plastic scrub brushes and floral-patterned oilcloth.

In the rapidly growing area of Latin American antiques and folk art, Martha Eagan has been a celebrated pioneer in the field. She is the author of two books on *milagros* and *reliquarios*, and her Pachamama Gallery in Santa Fe offers unique, hard-to-find Mexican elements and furniture, including religious artifacts, antique jewelry, and ceramics. The intriguing old-world flavor of her Canyon Road Gallery is echoed in her home, itself a collection of inspiring treasures—Mexican ranch tables as well as cedar trunks holding books, *santos*, and old Guatemalan textiles.

Opposite: A pine Chihuahua bed is at home with a colorful American quilt in Martha Eagan's guest bedroom.

A colorful room of folk-art treasures includes a painted pine bed from Zacatecas and a trunk and chair from Chihuahua.

"THE THING I LOVE MOST ABOUT MY BED IS ITS JOYFUL USE OF PAINT. IT SAYS QUINTESSENTIAL FOLK ART. THIS BED COULD BE AMERICAN, EUROPEAN, OR FROM ANY NUMBER OF PLACES, BUT THE PAINT— THAT MAKES IT MEXICAN!"
—MARTHA EAGAN

BEDROOMS

Until the turn of the century, the most common bed in Mexico was a portable *petate*, or woven reed mat. Rolled out onto the ground or atop benches, the *petate* is still a common sight in the countryside, often thrown over *camapecs* — long, slender ranch beds featuring a low arm on one side that serves as a headrest. The length of these ranch beds allows easy metamorphosis into coffee tables or casual benches with the addition of throw pillows. It is not untypical for traditional wedding processions to include a *petate*, customarily carried in the bridal party to symbolize the unity of bride and groom.

In coastal areas the *hamaca*, or hammock, is the most convenient, easily assembled, and ubiquitous sleeping sack. Dating from the sixteenth century, *hamacas* are widely seen in the marketplace, hanging on display in colorful rows, and are a common fixture in coastal homes or on sleepy portals. More than one person can fit in a hammock, as the matrimonial, or hammock for two, testifies.

Chihuahua and Zacatecas claim the most variations on the conventional bed. Many of the styles developed in these two states favor spindle or cutout headboards with boisterous, colorful designs in green, yellow, red, and blue. Although this more decorative style has attracted great interest in the United States market, the beds are most appropriate for children's or guest rooms because they were made in the smaller double size. The more standard, and ample, queen- and king-sized beds have been newly created in the style, fashioned from reclaimed Mexican woods and impressed with similar design schemes.

BATHROOMS

The compelling textures of old stone and wood have inspired a myriad of individual looks for contemporary bathrooms. In the Calderella house in El Paso, Texas, beautiful carved doors of this *alacena* open into hideaway storage for towels and soaps. Fitted inside a sized niche in the wall, this placement of the *alacena* conserves floor space. Small painted tables and chairs in the bathroom are easily arranged for relaxing.

In Ed Holler and Sam Saunders' Pátzcuaro home, accessing the bathroom through their old mesquite doors is a grand experience. Inside, hand-carved colonial stone basins are topped with high-tech faucets that spill water into the deep sinks, which over time have built up patinas that soften the look of the stone. For additional privacy, the commode has been placed in a closet-sized room, reached through another pair of mesquite-paneled doors.

In the home of a Santa Fe designer, a modern master bath with handmade tiles, jacuzzi, and steambath also give necessity to storage for large towels. A built-in closet was faced with a pair of colonial carved-cypress doors, adding a dimension of age to this contemporary bathroom.

An *alacena*, or built-in cabinet, from Durango adds charm to the bathroom of the Calderella house in El Paso, Texas.

Opposite: A colonial stone basin is topped with high-tech faucets in the Pátzcuaro home of Ed Holler and Sam Saunders.

GARDEN SPACES

Mexican elements are equally at home outdoors—adding shape and a comfortable weathered presence to gardens, courtyards, and sleepy portals. Milking stools and simple slab benches are now permanent fixtures in favorite garden corners. Having lived for years outside as solely utilitarian pieces, barn doors, corral gates, watering troughs, and various agricultural implements now enjoy nature with a new decorative posture.

On Florida's Hibiscus Island, graphic designers Jack and Claudia Auger have placed large coffee *morteros* amidst their tropical garden and have easily mixed their collection of Mexican painted tables with accents

A simple bench and potted plants surround this tranquil fountain courtyard.

and textiles collected from their travels in Bali and Hong Kong. Avid entertainers, they often bring their painted pieces outdoors for twilight dinners on their waterfront patio. The table's worn painted surfaces work well against

Opposite: Natural geodes add a contemporary touch to this outdoor patio overlooking Lake Pátzcuaro.

81

the textured peach walls of their Mediterranean-style home. Their tables also play host to their visually stimulating displays of fruits and delicacies.

Prior to their present redemption as flower planters, *bebederos*, or carved troughs, held livestock feed on ranches in northern and central Mexico. The yokes that once strapped the oxen are decorative as hanging

The "chapel" doors open to reveal a potting shed, replete with hanging tools, Mexican painted trunks, and a *trastero*, a reminder not to judge a gardener by his toolshed.

planters—perfect for supporting potted plants. Old filter stands—once holding stone filters that purified water—now display Mexican ceramics and accompany painted benches and coffee mortars on portals.

In desert gardens, on tropical patios, or inside courtyards and stair-wells, the furniture, vessels, and implements of Old Mexico inspire the

Opposite: James Havard's backyard "chapel" with large mesquite doors evokes a heaven-on-earth presence.

natural beauty of a space, inviting quiet contemplation or spirited conversation. With every outdoor occasion one couple hosts, they choreograph new

A painted table from Zacatecas doubles as a favorite breakfast spot on a portal overlooking the mountains around Oaxaca. Home of Rene Bustamente and Ann Miller.

Opposite: An old mesquite carpenter's bench keeps company with a large hollowed agave heart in the courtyard of the MorDō Ranch in Scottsdale, Arizona.

arrangements of their carved wooden stools, as eager to delight themselves as well as their guests who share in the appreciation of the shifting dances presented by the stools' odd, organic, whimsical shapes. A misshapen tree

A Tarahumara pot now sits where a filter stone once belonged on this water filter stand from Durango. A pot was usually situated below to catch the filtered water from the stone. Collection of Ron and Suzie Dubin.

Opposite: A slat-back cypress bench sits unused on a cold winter day on the portal of Bart and Brenda Jacobs in Santa Fe, New Mexico.

knot that once appeared as a sand crab returns for an encore—seen from another angle—as a walking spider.

Old jail doors have become ideal garden gates, and carpenters' benches are robust enough to make perfect potting surfaces. Throughout

the country, floral and garden stores especially are creating unique uses for these elements—displaying bulbs in large dough bowls and paper white narcissi in feeding troughs. One-of-a-kind pieces can be seen in such shops as San Francisco's The Gardener, Chicago's Urban Gardener, and Philadelphia's Yard Company. Each of these retailers make good use of the shapes and textures of vessels and objects.

COMMERCIAL & OFFICE SPACES

Adding intrigue to the world of visual display, Mexican country elements invite recognition in the window and floor displays of prominent specialty stores, lobbies of hotels, and dining rooms of restaurants.

Beginning in the late eighties, the Banana Republic stores used Mexican country pieces to present and accent their appealing apparel. Seeking to avoid prefabricated and mass-marketed display ware, visual merchandisers embraced the qualities of permanence, durability, and simplicity evoked by the antique pieces. Long, broad surface areas of mesquite and *sabino* tables were ideal for stacking and displaying sweaters, pants, and shirts, the richness of the old woods complementing the textures in the clothing. Accents such as old doors, hand-carved wooden bowls, mortars, benches, copper vessels, and stone basins provided innovative receptacles for smaller merchandise.

On the culinary front, Mexican vessels and implements are also present in culinary specialty stores, and are sought by catering professionals. Keeping company with other global treasures at Culinary Bazaar in Coral Gables, Florida, Mexican water jugs, sugar molds, and tortilla presses share window space with colorful milk cans from Colombia, Turkish copper pots, and Early American ladles and spoons. Equally attractive to catering professionals and set decorators, the utilitarian forms and objects have become popular as decorative accents for festive party displays, adding old-world charm to many special occasions.

Graduated sizes of *bateas* are stacked on the kitchen counter ready to be used as serving trays.

Opposite: Mexican country elements—a tree-stump stool, *morteros*, and *manos*—keep company with culinary antiques from around the world: cylindrical yogurt-making vessels from India, painted Colombian milk cans, Panamanian candy molds, fudge-stirring implements, and all-American spoons and spatulas. Culinary Bazaar, Coral Gables, Florida.

Santa Fe's luxury club community, Las Campanas, highlights The Hacienda with Mexican elements adding warmth and texture to the club's grand interior. The entrance hall features a ten-foot Mexican bench, which

A large coffee mortar adds texture to a ranch table display in a Banana Republic store.

sits comfortably under a painting entitled *When Santa Fe Was a Mexican Town*. Their dining room and gallery also feature painted *trasteros* and trunks. Also in Santa Fe, the Inn of the Anasazi, a world-class luxury hotel known for its warm, inviting lobby and fireplace, has guests gathering around a robust, Mexican-door coffee table that is the central focus of the room. House phones rest on simple ranch tables, and painted trunks add color to bedroom suites.

An old colonial stone feeding trough becomes an innovative display accent in the hands of creative Banana Republic designers.

The library of collector and artist Lee Nichols features a large mesquite table in the Washington, D.C., estate of Senator and Mrs. John D. Rocke-feller, IV. Nichols, majordomo of the estate, has traveled extensively through-out Mexico, and his collections of Mexican folk art and old dance masks are displayed artfully throughout his apartment. His eclectic collection also features a group of eighteenth-century hand-tooled-leather book covers, housed in a display created by Nichols from a fragment of a fine antique mirror.

Creatively arranged, Mexican country elements can collaborate to bring aesthetic flavor to a room. As a Oaxacan *mole* sauce derives its flavor from a combination of both old and new ingredients—nuts, spices, meats, and sesame seeds with foodstuffs of the New World such as chiles, tomatoes, and squash—so do age-old Mexican antiques unite seamlessly with modern

Comfortable and inviting, an old mesquite door rests in front of leather chairs as a table in the lobby of the Inn of the Anasazi, Santa Fe, New Mexico.

Opposite: A painted Mexican bench in the Hacienda Club at Las Campanas, a luxury club community in Santa Fe, New Mexico. Painting: *When Santa Fe Was a Mexican Town*, by William Ahrendt.

design accents. The word *mole* comes from the Nahuatl word meaning "concoction," and indeed, views of the design schemes of homeowners utilizing Mexican country furniture and elements bespeak unity in apparently disparate elements. The results of their design concoctions are both impressive and original, and testify to the possibilities for creative juxtapositions between old and new, simple and sophisticated.

Beautiful lustrous hardwoods, handwrought iron and copper, stone in many unusual hues—from pink to gray to green—all blend in limitless mixtures with today's contemporary settings. A mesquite coffee mortar is

paired effortlessly with a chrome and leather Mies Van der Rohe chair. Old colonial doors built into a living-room wall open to reveal a state-of-the-art entertainment center. Translucent, round, gear-shift knobs containing religious icons are piled into an ancient *batea* accenting a turned-leg dining table once used by Mexican customs agents to clear travelers headed south. A large, globe-shaped birdcage made of scrap iron is now wired with electricity

A classic Mexican table is at home in Ralph Lauren's New York design offices, providing a timeless elegance to the office of Buffy Birrittella, senior vice president of Advertising and Women's Design.

Opposite: A large mesquite table is the focal point in the library of collector and artist Lee Nichols in the Washington, D.C., estate of Senator and Mrs. John D. Rockefeller IV. Nichols, majordomo of the estate, displays his treasured hammered-tin candelabra from Guanajuato atop of a Guatemalan shaman's belt. Mexican masks posture nearby on antique hat stands.

and topped with a fiesta-blue linen lampshade. A stone water filter now spills over with ivy in a pool-side setting. Trunks and tortilla tables, once a part of every Mexican household, are now in new homes where they support dramatic modern lamps next to beds or line art-filled hallways. The examples are endless as designers find new uses for furniture and utilitarian elements highlighting the interest in creative restoration and recycling.

BUYING &
RESTORING

BECAUSE NO TWO BUYING TRIPS ARE ALIKE, BUYERS SHOULD HAVE THE PLEASURE OF BEING

surprised almost everywhere they go. As the locals say about travel and buying in Mexico, *"si*

no tienes paciencia, no tendras suerte," or "if you don't have patience, you don't have luck." More

often than not, discoveries have been made in unlikely settings and contexts, usually amidst col-

orful contrasts that one might find hard to imagine. Indeed, luck will increase in proportion to

the buyer's patience, and over time, patience will be well rewarded as unusual antique finds

evolve from dusty, forgotten relics to contemporary centerpieces rich with character and history.

Hand-created, these elements possess a texture and feel that machines can't duplicate.

Yet as lovers of Mexican artifacts connect to the nostalgia of these pieces, modern-day influ-

ences are fast encroaching on Mexico's remote rural villages. Modern metal-style doors and

tables, now regarded by many Mexicans as more secure, durable, and up-to-date, are replac-

ing weathered antiques. As Mexico looks toward the twenty-first century, progress has been

measured by tremendous urbanization. The rebuilding of old towns and the establishment of

new developments is the driving force behind the recent boom in the Mexican salvage busi-

ness. Many items are purchased directly from Mexican antique dealers and do not require

extensive restoration, merely a washing and waxing. However, the majority of elements

An intriguing pile of antique treasures—coffee mortars, shutters and doors—in the yard of antique dealer Alicia Castillo.

The turned legs of an old table have been saved for a future reincarnation.

Opposite: Coauthor Joe Carr and a restoration expert discuss Mexican hardwoods.

imported to the United States are acquired from salvage dealers and small businesses where the pieces have sat idle in stables, tack rooms, or outbuildings, long since retired from daily use because of missing drawers, damaged stretchers or legs, or simply because the owner preferred something else. Considering that many of the pieces we found date from the colonial period through the late 1800s, their survival (or in some cases, partial survival) in these conditions is a testament to the durability of the indigenous hardwoods and the skillful hands of the *carpinteros* who made them.

The finds of antique dealers are often weathered specimens that survive as modest symbols of their former lives and uses. Once transferred to vacant storage lots, the pieces are then acquired by furniture dealers and enterprising individuals, and stored in a variety of bodegas and warehouses. A bodega in Mexico quite often translates to any number of places that have extra space—barns, abandoned maize cribs, extra rooms in houses, and even auto junkyards, where fine old wooden doors are often stacked alongside salvaged car doors. In addition to furniture and agricultural implements, found elements include the dismantled architectural remains of old buildings, such as stone column bases, vigas, corbels, lintels with cutouts for pintle hinges, stone arcades and iron pediments, window guards, balcony balustrades, doorjambs, and ornamental accents.

Unlike traditional American antiques, which are sought for their pristine condition, Mexican antiques are coveted for their imperfections. The restoration of Mexican furniture—both native and recent—is common, and in many ways adds to the value and enjoyment of the pieces. *La cosa tiene mas miga de lo que parece*, or "there is more than meets the eye," is a familiar slang phrase used to refer to Mexican furniture in its weathered state. Artfully handcrafted, these pieces are deserving of a second chance and are made ready for their new extended lives through thoughtful restoration. By adapting to fresh functions and decorative new contexts, their cultural traditions are being kept alive.

Through time, one can train the eyes to look beneath the surface, allowing worn and idle objects, deceptively imperfect at first glance, to

become appealing. After years of undertaking the restoration process, experience will allow for recognition of specific wood characteristics and pieces with exceptional quality. Sometimes an item may be charming, but if it requires too much repair or too many replacement pieces, its restoration may be more costly than its value. If such items are priced well, they can be purchased and set aside for later use on more valuable pieces. Many a new table leg has been fashioned from an old mesquite doorjamb, just as an old table with a warped top might be purchased for its sturdy base to replace the badly burned base of another otherwise perfect tabletop.

A simple mesquite child's chair is pictured in its found condition. Collection of Tony Piraino.

Opposite: Old mesquite doors await conversion to coffee tables at Jack Calderella's El Paso workshop.

On one scouting trip in Mexico City, some antique dealers were asked by an enterprising taxi driver what kind of business they were in. Upon hearing their answer, he asked if they would like to see some old tables. Making a quick 180-degree turn, he drove the dealers to the local bullring while mentioning that his brother ran the place and that the bullring's old ticket-taking tables were just recently replaced with new metal

100

styles. "Where were the old ones?" the buyers wondered. They should have known—in a dark basement closet that sat conveniently under the howling, stomping crowds of the bullring. The beam of a flashlight illuminated a matching pair of hearty mesquite tables in perfectly squared proportions, ticket stubs still scattered in the only remaining drawer. Inspecting closely for recent repairs, the buyers were amused to find that the original wooden

drawer pull had been replaced with a familiar-looking, round Lucite knob encasing a mini-portrait of Our Lady of Guadalupe—the same image beaming from the sparkling knobs of the taxi driver's radio dials and pop-up door locks! Their business for the day had suddenly come full circle, lit-erally. They purchased the tables because of their age and sturdy construction, and the only real repair required was to replace one drawer.

A colorful old barber's chair shows potential.

Opposite: Two examples of old colonial doors with simple decorative carving.

In the many hours they have spent stranded on Mexican streets patiently waiting for a resource to unearth his keys to a nearby bodega or storehouse, these same dealers confess they have acquired a taste for *chicharrones*, or fried pork rinds, and Fanta, a close cousin of orange Crush, making do with what is for sale in the barrio, or neighborhood, usually from street vendors. On one occasion, while waiting on a street corner, they were amused by a painted rock at a bus stop; it had been transformed into a colorful checkerboard, complete with a nearby stash of red and blue bottle caps to be used as game pieces. Inventiveness is everywhere in Mexico—one need only look closely to find it. The dealers' eventual entry to the Aguascalientes storeroom in this case didn't turn up much, but they had an interesting discovery at a cantina a few doors down where they spotted an old wooden barber chair whose headrest was adjustable via a wooden peg. An inviting favored seat at the head of the cantina's bar, it was understandably treasured by its owner and therefore not for sale.

Sometimes dealers are shown rooms stacked to the ceiling with trunks, or hallways lined ten-deep with old doors. With a jumble of potential antique treasures competing for their attention, they must let their eyes relax and slowly gaze through the piles. They assess items initially by shape and size, surveying a room or a stack, looking for interesting lines and proportions. Most seasoned dealers' eyes usually gravitate to pieces that are sculptural and not necessarily functional—a large piece of wood carved in a Y-shape, say, with a square hole cut in its center. Though the original use is now forgotten, its warm patina testifies to years of heavy use, making it a choice candidate for a stand-alone sculpture in a contemporary setting.

Part of the value in Mexican antique furniture is expressed in signs of many roles and many owners. Often self-taught, many carpenters made up for the absence of fine tools by using the natural aberrations of beautiful woods to make individual statements. In this way, knot holes sometimes

102

A mesquite tabletop features a simple plug to replace a hole in the wood. Antique Warehouse, Santa Fe, New Mexico.

Opposite: A native repair on a mortar features a tin patch.

become a table's punctuation. Traces of paint are often found on the pieces, as are carved initials of old sweethearts or numbers commemorating significant dates. Doors that have withstood decades of weather—with painted surfaces faded to shades one only wishes he could duplicate, their hardware pitted and rusted and later polished by use—still maintain their strength and authority.

Old storage trunks for clothing and personal belongings often have paper prayer cards pasted to the inside lids and are sometimes lined with faded floral paper or remnants of found magazine pages. Inside one trunk, Our Lady of Guadalupe prayer cards were pasted alongside tattered magazine reviews of films featuring Madonna and Clint Eastwood.

Some of the coveted, more unusual pieces include tables with single-slab mesquite or *sabino* tops—often over six feet long and twenty-six inches wide. Impressive and robust in size and handsomely proportioned, these tables usually have A-frame bases, and their tabletops are considered rare wood specimens. The older, better pieces have original *clavos*, or large-headed nails, on top. Other sought-after pieces are colonial-style benches with either spindle or slat backs and graceful arms, desks with original drawers and unusual *faldons*, or skirts, as well as elegant *armarios*, or armoires, with cutout *copetes*, or crests, and distinctive painted surfaces. Even reclaimed molding and balcony balustrades—lengths that were not damaged by wear or fire— can be salvaged and designed into large-scale mirror frames.

Choice finds include those with original hardware and tables with original drawers. Hand-hewn woods are also high on the list of favorites, as are pieces with rare joinery and unique dimensions. In general, dealers look for pleasing proportions, beautiful hardwoods, and innovative techniques of the craftsmen. Indeed, one reason a great deal of this furniture is still available for refurbishing is that they were so well made, having been crafted of durable hardwoods such as mesquite, *sabino*, and heart pine that were allowed to dry naturally for long periods of time before being hand-dressed.

An old mesquite ranch table, deceptively unattractive in its weathered state, will soon be cleaned and restored for a new extended life.

Opposite: The difference between waxed and unwaxed mesquite doors is evident.

Often when buying *morteros* and *bateas*, the first thing seen is their undersides. Stacked in large piles upside down, they reveal odd tin patches hammered into places where the wood has begun to split. Larger pieces are patched with almost anything handy—old license plates, iron hinges, and even rubber shoe heels.

Most items are found in a disguised state, with layers of dirt and paint hiding their beauty and appeal. Because they're not instantly recognizable as worth saving, it is necessary to carry some sleuthing tools to help detect a quality piece worthy of renovation. A close inspection of weathered Mexican antiques is usually accompanied by the ritual opening of a pocketknife, indispensable for nicking paint layers to access and determine the kind of wood. It is also a good idea to carry water bottles. Water can be used to wet down an area of the silvered wood, as wet wood simulates the darkened tone it may resemble when waxed.

To the enlightened renovator, everything can have a second life, and that life, freed from the constraints of context, is often richer than the first. This is certainly the case with the handcrafted pieces found in weathered or neglected states of disrepair that have proudly endured candle burn marks, worn-out knotholes, and gouges, not to mention the caress of loving hands.

There are great benefits inherent in closely combing over every inch of a piece. While washing away layers of time and grease, one has the opportunity to discover whimsical details and remnants of history in hidden corners and the undersides of boards. The complex appeal of wear marks and age include multiple layers of old paint, surfaces that have been personalized with cattle brands, native repairs done with tin or rawhide straps, old nails, worn edges, and primitive-looking iron hardware.

Over the years, some antique dealers assemble their own extensive photographic archive of before-and-after shots of the pieces they have

found and restored, allowing them to accurately predict what an item will resemble when it's finished and waxed. A record of hundreds of timeworn pieces, the archive can document the metamorphosis from weathered to restored and celebrated. Photographic documentation of the steps in the

A painted trunk was found lined with floral wallpaper.

Opposite: An antique dealer's warehouse contains a colorful collection of old trunks.

restoration process enhances a client's understanding and appreciation of a particular piece's life. The photographs often show the piece's original uses and weathered states before restoration, as well as revealing archaic construction methods and charming details from former lives.

An old mesquite carpenter's bench has survived the wear and tear of many projects. The rectangular hole once held a toolbox.

Opposite: The Castillo carpentry shop in Mexico.

To sustain the original charm of a piece in the restoration process, one needs an imaginative set of hands paired with dedication and the time to roll up one's sleeves. Very simply, the transformation process is hard work, but it is a labor of love. Often what is needed is only a basic soap-and-water washing, but more often than not, the process is arduous and time-consuming— and laden with grime and dirt.

Mesas de carniceros, or butcher tables/meat display tables, bearing chop marks are usually the most challenging to restore since meat residue tends to harden over time. Trisodium phosphate (TSP) is often necessary in order to easily strip away its layers. Tables used in the marketplace sometimes have telltale signs of their previous incarnations too—seeds are still visible in crevices and staples lurk under a tabletop's edges, evidence of its former oilcloth cover.

The journey from a forgotten bodega in Mexico to a contemporary home in the United States involves a complex choreography of steps. A great deal of patience and foresight is required, as well as an understanding of import/export regulations and restoration techniques.

After purchasing and labeling the items, dealers often hire a local truck to pick up their finds and transport them to a Mexican trucking company. Delicate pieces must first be taken to a packing company or, better yet, packed by the buyers for extra assurance.

The pieces usually travel close to 600 miles out of central Mexico before they reach the United States border. Once at the border, a Mexican export broker must be consulted in order to guide the shipment through the maze of paperwork required to pass through United States Customs. After still more paperwork is filed with an American import broker and the load is cleared by customs, it must be transferred to another truck hired to take the shipment to its final American destination. Once unloaded, the restoration process begins.

Layered with dirt and encrusted paint, the pieces must first undergo a thorough washing to expose the beautiful woods that lie beneath. In going over every inch of the piece, problem areas are detected and a plan of action emerges as to which method of restoration will be best for the final desired results. In some cases original paint is left; in others, it is entirely stripped.

With pieces painted several times over, it is also possible to remove just a few layers of paint, retaining a hint of an earlier hue.

It is often necessary to tighten loose mortise-and-tenon joints and inspect surfaces for need of patching, strengthening, or replacing old nails.

Restorers keep an extensive collection of old square-head nails and *clavos* close at hand to match missing elements.

Most antique dealers and restorers favor Minwax paste wax in both light and dark varieties. It is a rich wax that, when applied and buffed, gives a lustrous polish and adds depth to the color of the wood. Its properties allow for a strong buildup, requiring about two to three coats for a base. Certainly any quality paste wax will do the job; however, industry experts prefer the effects of Minwax.

Many smaller pieces can be taken on easily as first-time projects. *Bateas*, milking stools, grain-storage boxes, and even carved wooden shoe forms make fun starts to test different methods and define one's feel for the handwork. Not all finds are 100 percent wood elements; dealers may also purchase large copper bowls and pitchers that need special copper polish. Wrought-iron window guards or balcony railings have required special treatments as well.

Each buying trip brings a new challenge and a new result. As one can imagine, techniques of restoration vary and involve not just sweat but ingenuity. The journey from weathered to renewed is an intimate one. Involved in every stage, antique dealers and restorers feel great satisfaction in recycling elements so full of history and life. Many pieces are deserving of a second chance as they were crafted with a great design sense and have a wealth of character beneath the layers of mud, lard, or food residues. Indeed, it is often the long, multifaceted journey of restoration that adds such great value and revives the soul of these fine old pieces.

Detail of carved wooden door and *clavos*.

Opposite: A stairwell of old iron treasures awaits buyers in Mexico.

TIPS FOR BUYING

Inspect the overall construction. Make sure wood braces aren't cracked or broken. Take a door and set it on its edge. With your eyes close to one end, inspect for a straightness to ensure it isn't warped. Even though pieces are predominately hardwoods, long exposure to harsh elements can cause warping and wood rot. Check for insect damage and inspect edges for dry rot or extensive water exposure; also, look for loose corner joints or missing hinges. Doors with missing or damaged inner panels can have the panels removed and replaced with newly crafted panels for a contemporary old-new combination.

Loose joints can be tightened, but split wood and broken joints are more difficult to repair. When inspecting, press down on the top and move the piece from side to side to see if the mortise-and-tenon joints are loose. This is especially common in very old pieces in which the wood shrinks over time and causes joints to separate slightly and wiggle loose. This is not an obstacle; they are easily shimmed and made sturdy again, and are indeed one of the telltale determinants of an item's age. In Mexico, a common temporary fix for loose mortise and tenons is to drive large nails into the table or bench top or directly into the mortise and tenon. Over a period of eighty years or so, one piece could have been host to many nails, eventually resulting in split wood. With pieces like these, remove the nails where the wood has split. Inject glue in their places and clamp the pieces back together. When dry, place a countersink below the surface and drive a screw from the top down into the base. On top of this, add a short wooden dowel to hide the metal screw.

If a table is wobbly from a loose mortise and tenon, or if either the tenon has snapped or one top board has split, an easy way to salvage the table is to chop it down to a narrower width by cutting the skirt and stretchers—if still present.

The old mortise can still be used for the new dimensions; however, new tenons must be cut. Missing or broken stretchers can easily be replaced to brace the legs, providing more function and durability. Tables with a hole on top can be fixed by designing a newly shaped plug for the hole, such as a heart or other whimsical shape.

SHIPPING/CUSTOMS/BROKERS

Once items are acquired, it is necessary to become familiar with the laws governing the export and import of furniture from Mexico into the United States. In a majority of cases, there is no import duty, but there will be normal customs entrance fees as well as the need for a Mexican export broker and a United States import broker. As far as shipping is concerned, almost everything moves by truck, and some trucking firms are more reliable and careful with your merchandise than others.

RESTORATION

Working with Mexican furniture and architectural fragments allows you to see potential in the unexpected. A creative imagination proves valuable. However, in order to gain the knowledge necessary to train your eye, nothing beats hands-on experience—the washing, scouring, and burnishing with steel wool, and waxing—that yields insight for quality finds worth revitalizing. A close look both inside and out is necessary to find the subtle details or deviations in construction or native repairs that reveal telltale signs of its original use. All of these add to a piece's character.

Many times you can approach antique dealers to buy pieces in their weathered, unrestored states straight off their trucks from Mexico. This allows you to experience the restoration process personally and to customize your antiques to your own specifications while becoming more familiar with the intricacies of restoration.

The simple process of washing old weathered wood is the most essential element in reviving this kind of furniture. As most durable pieces were crafted from Mexican hardwoods—mesquite, *sabino*, heart pine, or mahogany—their colorful richness can be brought to life with soap, water, and a little determination. The befores and afters can be strikingly different.

PRESERVING THE PATINA

After many years of restoring Mexican country antiques, the question most often asked is, "How do you get such an appealing finish (or patina) on your furniture?" The warm, rich glow of the wood surfaces draws people close, tapping something inside, inspiring a hands-on, tactile inspection. This first intimate encounter is one of our favorite steps in the entire process.

1. Since most antiques are shipped by truck, it is necessary to remove the road grime and dirt. Almost every piece, with a few exceptions, must be washed on arrival. This is done best with a light solution of trisodium phosphate (TSP) and warm water mixed together in a bucket. Use of a scrub brush ensures removal of unwanted excess oils, meat residues, and built-up dirt.

2. After washing, rinse the piece off with clean water and let it dry fully. A fine-grade steel wool is then used to take off any lingering dirt or loose paint. Do not use sandpaper for this purpose because it will remove the original patina and leave an uneven color on the wood.

3. Once this step is finished, it is necessary to protect the surface and bring out the true color of the wood by applying one to three coats of Minwax paste wax. If you are working with light-colored woods, use the natural variety. If you're working with dark woods, especially mesquite, use the dark-tinted wax. First apply the wax with a soft rag, making sure it gets into all the cracks and crevices. Let dry for fifteen minutes. Buff with a clean rag and then repeat. You will obtain a high-gloss, lasting shine that adds depth to the color of the wood.

PREPARING TABLES AND BENCHES FOR OUTDOOR USE

For an outdoor finish, use a water-soluble sealant to preserve the natural color of the wood and protect it from the elements. A water-soluble sealant will give a matte finish. After cleaning the wood surface, use a brush to apply the milky-colored sealant. It has a self-leveling agent so that it won't leave brush marks, and it dries quickly in approximately thirty minutes. Follow this stage with a fine steel wool to smooth out any rough parts, then repeat two to three times. Each coat will provide a smoother finish.

STAIN REMOVAL

For water stains, wipe the area clean with a damp cloth. Using a pad of fine steel wool, rub the stained area in a circular motion. After you have eliminated the stain, go over the entire area lightly with the steel wool, then apply a coat of wax. Oxalic acid, widely used for cleaning decks, is useful in removing mildew stains and is available in most hardware stores. Used in a mild solution, it will gently lighten the color of the wood and remove the mildew stain.

PAINT STRIPPING

We recommend professional paint stripping when a painted piece of furniture needs to be stripped, for example when you want to return the piece to its natural wood state. Preferably it should be hand-stripped as opposed to being dipped or tank soaked. Tank stripping not only exposes you to toxic fumes but also tends to dry out the wood and, hence, weaken joints or repairs that have been glued. Overall, hand-stripping does less harm and, even though more costly, it saves having to re-repair loose joints or older repairs. Professionals also have the ability to safely dispose of caustic stripping agents.

CONTEMPORARY ADAPTATIONS

AS THE POPULARITY OF MEXICAN COUNTRY DESIGN STYLES HAS GROWN, THE INCREASED

demand has limited the availability of existing antiques, resulting in new developments in the

consumer market. People who are now unable to find an authentic antique piece or who are

simply attracted to the newer adapted styles have accepted the quality reproductions, especially

those crafted from reclaimed Mexican wood elements.

Recycling wood products is a key element in the push towards resource conservation, but

there's an aesthetic factor also to be considered. Reusing wood and accessory materials as well

as metal and stone from older structures can lend the new application visual and textural

integrity that would otherwise take years to achieve. One of the reasons today's design scene

has so many creative applications is that these elements adapt easily to contemporary functions

and artful atmospheres. Old gates and *moldes de azucar* can be used as tables and headboards,

while pairs of doors can be used to make armoires to house entertainment units. A mesquite

ranch table once used in the marketplace took on a new role as a prominent display table for

sweaters in a Banana Republic store. Pot racks once used for storing *ollas*, or ceramic water

pots, are now used as decorative racks for flowerpots. Wheel hubs and storage jars have

A colonial mesquite door with iron finials makes its way into a New York bedroom as a headboard. Large *clavos* and remains of old *gozne* hinges recall its previous utilitarian life. A nineteenth-century *molde de azucar* stands close by as a cherished design accent.

evolved into simple lamp bases, and coffee mortars now hold abundant displays of dried flowers. Cheese presses without their vices and screw nuts make side tables with the addition of iron bases.

Moreover, today's living and entertaining standards have inspired homeowners and designers to seek specific size requirements for functional furniture with an old-world look. The market has responded to this desire by producing pieces in dimensions that better suit today's interior design choices. Specifically, contemporary armoires are made deep enough to house televisions, and door headboards are available to fit king-size beds. Old doors are being modified in a variety of ways to hold court in the center of living rooms and dens as coffee tables, a kind of furniture uncommon in old-world Mexico.

Certain modifications involve essentially recycling pieces; with creativity, a damaged item can be adjusted and reinvented for a new life. A table with a portion of its top damaged can be "cut down" or reduced in width to become functional as a narrow hallway or entrance table. Tables with damaged legs can be shortened to become bedside tables or coffee tables. A door frame with a missing interior panel can be transformed into a mirror frame. A table with side rails can be altered by moving stretchers to the center, allowing for proper foot space in a dining capacity. All of these examples make new use of pieces and still convey an antique presence without appearing replicated.

Consumers are fascinated with antique styles because of their age, quality, and unique beauty. Between the old and the newly adapted is the human element, which allows contemporary adaptations to belong to the past while being imbued with modern creativity and spirit.

In many cases today, entire lines of contemporary furniture are being produced from the recovered remains of antique pieces and architectural elements. This approach to renovation is more about overall rebirth than

A very rare, eleven-foot-long single-slab of *sabino*, or Mexican cypress, was found by the authors in the state of Jalisco. Collection of Karen Vaughan Productions.

Opposite: A grouping of contemporary tables were made from mesquite, cypress, and cottonwood by Joe P. Carr and David Martinez.

repair. Old shutters and doors no longer in use are the raw materials for armoires, serving tables, chests of drawers, desks, and nightstands. A very time-consuming technique, this work requires craftsmen to meticulously match wood surfaces to individual pieces, thus creating uniformity in color and pattern.

The recovering and recycling of unusual wood specimens has been a focus of the Carr-Wit Design Studio in recent years. The studio has received unusual requests from architects and interior designers who have admired the unusually thick slab-top worktables discovered by Carr-Wit in Mexico but have begun requesting similar styles in harder-to-find sizes—dining tables that could seat twelve or round tables to fit unusual kitchen spaces.

Since round tables were not widely produced in Mexico, and extremely long tables over seven feet are difficult to find today, Carr-Wit began designing contemporary styles from old reclaimed wood to suit the designers' specifications. Many styles followed old colonial examples, some featuring *mariposa*, or butterfly, joinery for table surfaces along with simple squared legs or the more traditional lyre-leg base. Working predominately in mesquite and *sabino*, Carr-Wit Studio often took its cue for these custom tables from the rare individual wood specimens uncovered on dormant ranches.

Large pairs of doors are now more likely to become either dining tables or headboards with the addition of clean-lined contemporary iron bases and iron finials. The simplicity of the iron complements the warmth of the old wood, a comfortable coexistence in contemporary interiors. For more traditional design environments, Carr-Wit's custom harvest tables in eight-foot lengths feature old planks and bases crafted from centuries-old vigas or from antique doorjambs. Drawers for these tables have even been made from salvaged raised-door panels. Even old iron birdcages and water filter stands can be converted into floor lamps.

120

In the last few years, there has been a surge of creativity involving the use of ox yokes as table bases. The development of the ox-yoke table began in the workshops of Texas border towns, and its adaptations spread quickly throughout the country. As advanced machinery on farmlands made thousands of ox yokes obsolete, the *yugos*, or yokes, of Mexico first found their

way into American homes in the Southwest as decorative accents over doorways or fireplace mantels.

Their newfound use as table legs and center stretchers combines both function and aesthetics with the yokes' hand-carved shapes serving as wonderful complements to the single-panel doors that form their table-tops. A variety of styles are available from designers and antique dealers.

As an importer of Mexican country antiques and the designer of a number of handsome reproductions, Jack Dulaney of El Paso Imports has attracted national attention with his contemporary door tables and his newly interpreted *mesa de carnicero*, sometimes referred to simply as a *carniceria* table. Its original construction features a support beam that allows meats to be hung from hooks and displayed over the tabletop.

An ox-yoke table greets visitors in the Eldorado Hotel, Santa Fe, New Mexico. Design by Foreign Traders.

Opposite: A grand-scale *ropero* of antique pine and hardwood retains its original paint patina. Design by Foreign Traders.

Crafted from old Mexican woods, Dulaney's *carniceria* tables are an antique style that has won favor with consumers and is easily adapted to modern use in kitchens as decorative prep stations. The original meat hooks now sport strings of chiles, gourds, garlic strands, or pots and pans. This unique piece features old wood and has the modern-day benefit of a newly added drawer for utensils. Once again, it is an element unavailable in large quantities as an antique but whose reproductions have been popular in the contemporary market.

A coffee mortar in sculptor Judith Simpson's Philadelphia garden adds sculptural shape to her recycled iron sculptures. Her collection of cup-shaped mortars plays a variety of roles throughout the year. At Christmas, the mortars are filled with holly and white pine boughs, which take on welcoming personalities on either side of her front entrance.

Opposite: Adding an entirely new twist on the equipale, these chairs and tables are now carved meticulously out of stone for all-weather use in outdoor gardens. La Casa Canela, Tlaquepaque, Jalisco, Mexico.

While original doors can be converted into table surfaces, even old doors with damaged panels can be saved for contemporary table surfaces, with metal surfaces replacing the interior broken boards. Carr-Wit has designed variations that house perforated or punched steel within mesquite frames, and Jack Calderella of El Paso has crafted unique parquet tabletops in such frames. Remnants of old wood are assembled within the original door frame using varying shades of wood to create a contrasting, geometric design.

Alex Tschursin of Foreign Traders in Santa Fe produces the Hacienda Collection, whose pieces are characteristic of old Mexico's grand hacienda era. This unusual collection features richly textured hardwoods milled centuries ago that reflect the spirit of their original era. Handcrafted by the renowned Esteban Chapital, these reproductions are reminiscent of old design styles and incorporate historic details, including hand-forged iron hardware. The overall form and configuration of the styles is based on old Mexican pieces, yet their design details express artistic freedom. Influenced by the renowned Mexican architects Barragán and Legoretta, Chapital favors their same bold use of color and combinations in the assembly of original painted door panels for new armoires. Each piece takes on the unique attributes of its found materials and dismantled remains—antique doors, beams, rafters—and is transformed into a showpiece with a past. The woods used retain the original antique paint finish. After being cleaned and preserved, this color patina remains.

Numerous companies are producing creative interpretations of Mexico's popular basics, including the ever-present pigskin *equipale* chairs, which can now be found in new dimensions—love seats, bar stools, chaise lounges, and ottomans—and are covered in a variety of materials from suede and cowhide to custom fabrics and woven fibers. Adding an entirely new twist, these popular chairs and round tables are now carved meticulously out of stone for all-weather use in outdoor gardens.

Two of the most consistently innovative people in Mexican design are Ed Holler and Sam Saunders. With locations in Nogales, Arizona, and Morelia, Mexico, they are a special resource for Latin American furniture and have creatively adapted Mexican elements for contemporary use over many years. Today, their grand-scale pieces include *cajoneras*, or large fifteen-foot-long buffets with drawers, as well as large-scale mirrors and tables. Also notable is their collection of lamps made from colonial *mieleras*, or jars used in storage and shipping of sugarcane syrup, featuring silver-plated lamp shades.

Another source that has forged new ground by combining old artifacts with contemporary iron designs is Galeria San Ysidro in El Paso, Texas. In addition to an extensive line of iron lighting and accents, owner Harl Dixon designs custom iron bases for armoires and sculptural wood fragments brought to him by clients. Aged corbels and stone pediments are also turned into one-of-a-kind functional pieces with the addition of iron bases.

Old traditional elements have captivated us with their textures, colors, and woods, and have added dimension to our present lives. We have found ways to keep them alive by giving them newfound functions and making them relevant in our present-day environments.

The tremendous growth of this industry—producing contemporary reproductions from old Mexican elements—has given rise to more jobs and studios in both Mexico and the United States. The success of many prosperous operations has touched the lives of hundreds of Mexican craftsmen, improving their standard of living and allowing them to revive almost-forgotten skills, learn new methods, and be rewarded for their creativity.

The category of contemporary adaptations is continually changing as the creativity of craftsmen on both sides of the border adapts to invent new designs based on old-world styles and to find inspiration in reclaimed building materials.

126

This faux-grain painted pine *armario* features raised-panel doors and sides. The old base, long-since discarded, has been replaced by a wrought-iron design by Harl Dixon. Galeria San Ysidro Collection.

Opposite: Mesquite shoemaker's forms sit comfortably on a windowsill with an iron sculpture by Judith Simpson.

UNEXPECTED ACCENTS

THE ADDED ATTRACTION OF DECORATING WITH MEXICAN COUNTRY FURNITURE IS THE INFINITE variety of accessories that can provide warmth and personality to a room. Common gourds, mineral specimens, and old shoemaker's forms are just as appealing as the more traditional ceramics, baskets, and textiles. Simple objects of a kind, when grouped together in multiples, acquire a whole new decorative dimension. A row of old lock plates on a mantel or a threesome of fishing traps in a corner emphasize the subtle structural distinctions existing in a single form.

In our quest for unusual pieces, visits to Mexico's antique flea markets are inevitably fruitful. From old trunk keys and door hardware, to individual turned spindles removed from broken window guards, to hats and old masks—all have limitless design potential. Carved-wood ox yokes, wheel hubs, and worn butterfly nuts from old carpenter's benches radiate a time-honored presence and a handcrafted sincerity that allow them to hold their own in many modern interiors. Even a group of mesquite corral-gate hinges can lend an abstract touch to a textured wall.

The look can also be about mixing unusual fragments: new lucite religious gearshift knobs, perhaps displayed in a weathered mesquite *batea*, or hunks of selenite crystals can add intrigue to marble tabletops. The delight is often in how these objects hold our attention in new contexts,

Small stone mortars make a minimal statement atop a painted Zacatecas table. Collection of Karen Witynski and Joe P. Carr.

adding a refreshing flavor to our personal spaces. Even on a grand scale, an old carved sugarcane press works alone as an inviting accent in the open-air lobby of The Hotel Santa Fe in Puerto Escondido, Oaxaca.

The marketplace is our favorite spot for picking inspiring shapes and objects for use in thought-provoking juxtapositions. Perforated gourds that

Top: A Huastecan pot from San Luis Potosí sits atop three graduated cypress trunks from Jalisco.

Mexican dance masks are displayed next to a selenite crystal sculpture, *Crystal Boy*, by Joe P. Carr.

Opposite: Lucite gear shift knobs are a colorful contrast to an old mesquite *batea*. Carr-Wit Studio.

are sold as colanders can become vessels for holding dried flowers or, assembled in a group, can add an organic touch to bookshelves or mantels. The bold graphics of Oaxacan baskets call attention just as well atop kitchen cabinets as upon desks or tables supporting letters, photos, and the like. Volcanic rock *molcajetes* can still be used to grind chiles but will more likely be found holding collections of shells or bath beads, and wooden chocolate whisks easily become works of art when displayed in groupings.

130

RESOURCE GUIDE

We would like to share with you the following top American resources for Mexican country furniture, architectural elements, and accents.

We also invite you to view a behind-the-scenes look at the world of *Mexican Country Style* at our Web site: http://www.mexicanstyle.com. We welcome your comments and questions!

In addition to our selection of Mexican antiques and contemporary tables, we offer interior design services through our Carr-Wit Studio. Personalized antique buying tours of Mexico can also be arranged through our Texas office.

MEXICAN COUNTRY STYLE
Web site:
http://www.mexicanstyle.com

CARR-WIT
3267 Bee Caves Road #107
Austin, TX 78746
(512) 370-9663
(512) 328-2966 Fax

CARR-WIT
19 Railroad Avenue #212
East Hampton, NY 11937
(516) 548-8114
By Appointment

CARR-WIT
Antique Buying Tours of Mexico
Guadalajara, Mexico
(512) 370-9663 in Austin, TX

THE MEXICAN MUSEUM
Fort Mason Center
Laguna and Marina Boulevards
San Francisco, CA 94123
(415) 441-0445

RETAIL RESOURCES

ARIZONA

EL PASO IMPORTS
4750 N. 16th Street
Phoenix, AZ 85016
(602) 222-9932

HOLLER AND SAUNDERS
590 W. International Street
Nogales, AZ 85628
(520) 287-5153

HOLLER AND SAUNDERS
Alvaro Obregon 143
Morelia, Michoacán, Mexico
(52) 43 121752

MORNING STAR TRADERS
2020 E. Speedway
Tucson, AZ 85719
(520) 881-2112

TOTALLY SOUTHWEST
5575 E. River Road #131
Tucson, AZ 85750
(520) 577-2295

CALIFORNIA

ARTE DE MEXICO
1000 Chestnut Street
Burbank, CA 91506
(818) 753-4559

DESIGN CENTER INC.
2754 Calhoun Street
San Diego, CA 92110
(619) 298-1141

EL PASO IMPORTS
913 State Street
Santa Barbara, CA 93101
(805) 963-7530

EL PASO IMPORTS
811 University Avenue
Berkeley, CA 94703

FEDERICO
1522 Montana
Santa Monica, CA 90403
(310) 458-4134

GALISTEO
590 - 10th Street
San Francisco, CA 94103
(415) 861-5900

MIKE HASKELL
539 San Ysidro Road
Santa Barbara, CA 93108
(805) 565-1121

JIM JETER
P.O. Box 682
Summerland, CA 93067
(805) 969-6746

RITUALS
756 N. La Cienega
Los Angeles, CA 90069
(213) 854-0848

TAIL OF THE YAK
2632 Ashby
Berkeley, CA 94705
(510) 841-9891

THE GARDENER
1836 Fourth Street
Berkeley, CA 94710
(510) 548-6116

COLORADO

CRY BABY RANCH
1422 Larimer Square
Denver, CO 80202
(303) 623-3979

EL PASO IMPORTS
723 S. Broadway
Denver, CO 80209

ZONA
107 S. Mill Street
Aspen, CO 81611
(970) 925-3763

DISTRICT OF COLUMBIA

SANTA FE STYLE
1413 Wisconsin N.W.
Washington, DC 20007
(202) 333-3747

FLORIDA

CULINARY BAZAAR
254 Giralda
Coral Gables, FL 33132
(305) 448-6064

FOUR WINDS GALLERY
17 Fillmore
Sarasota, FL 34236
(941) 388-2510

ONLY YESTERDAY
6576 S.W. 40th Street
Miami, FL 33155
(305) 666-2585

SOUTHERN FINE ARTS
3070 S.W. 38th Avenue
Miami, FL 33146
(305) 446-1641

GEORGIA

NEW ENGLAND HOME
ANTIQUES
Appalachian Hwy. 515
Jasper, GA 30143
(404) 692-9491

ILLINOIS

URBAN GARDENER
1006 W. Armitage Avenue
Chicago, IL 60614
(773) 477-2070

MISSOURI

MATERIAL CULTURE
405 S. Lamar
Oxford, MO 38655
(601) 234-7055

NEW MEXICO

ANTIQUE WAREHOUSE
530 S. Guadalupe Street #B
Santa Fe, NM 87501
(505) 984-1159

CLAIBORNE GALLERY
608 Canyon Road
Santa Fe, NM 87501
(505) 982-8019

DWELLINGS REVISTED
10 Bent Street
Taos, NM 87571
(505) 758-3377

EL PASO IMPORTS
419 Sandoval Street
Santa Fe, NM 87501
(505) 982-5698

EL PASO IMPORTS
3500 Central Street
Albuquerque, NM 87106
(505) 265-1160

FOREIGN TRADERS
202 Galisteo Street
Santa Fe, NM 87501
(505) 983-6441

JOSHUA BAER
116 1/2 E. Palace
Santa Fe, NM 87501
(505) 988-8944

LA PUERTA
1302 Cerrillos Road
Santa Fe, NM 87501
(505) 984-8164

NONESUCH ART AND
ANTIQUES
By Appointment
Santa Fe, NM 87501
(505) 988-4002

RENE BUSTAMENTE
1700-B Lena Street
Santa Fe, NM 87505
(505) 988-7386

NEW YORK

ABC CARPET & HOME
888 Broadway
New York, NY 10023
(212) 473-3000

CARR-WIT
19 Railroad Avenue #212
East Hampton, NY 11937
(516) 548-8114
By Appointment

ZONA
97 Greene Street
New York, NY 10023
(212) 925-6750

OREGON

SIGNATURE IMPORTS
638 S.W. Alder
Portland, OR 97232
(503) 222-5340

PENNSYLVANIA

FOUR WINDS GALLERY
5512 Walnut Street
Pittsburgh, PA 15232
(412) 683-2895

YARD CO.
8430 Germantown Avenue
Philadelphia, PA 19118
(215) 247-3390

RHODE ISLAND

KAREN VAUGHAN
227 Coggeshall Avenue
Newport, RI 02840
(401) 846-4774

TEXAS

ANTIGUA
1505 S. Congress
Austin, TX 78704
(512) 912-1475

CARR-WIT
3267 Bee Caves Road #107
Austin, TX 78746
(512) 370-9663

CIERRA
5829 Kirby Drive
Houston, TX 77005
(713) 942-9001

CIERRA
5502 Burnett Road
Austin, TX 79756
(512) 454-8603

CIERRA
5154 Broadway
San Antonio, TX 78209
(210) 824-8899

EL PASO IMPORTS
311 Montana
El Paso, TX 79902
(915) 542-4241

EL PASO IMPORTS
4524 McKinney Avenue
Dallas, TX 75205
(214) 559-0907

EL VALLE GALLERY
10375 Socorro Road
Socorro, TX 79927
(915) 858-3340

GALERIA SAN YSIDRO
801 Texas Avenue
El Paso, TX 79917
(915) 544-4444

JACK CALDERELLA
5660 El Paso Drive
El Paso, TX 79905
(915) 772-2779

OSCAR'S ANTIQUES
1002 Guadalupe
Laredo, TX 78040
(210) 723-0765

ROBERT KRASEY
10746 Limas Drive
El Paso, TX 79935
(915) 593-8469

TINHORN TRADERS
1608 S. Congress Avenue
Austin, TX 78704
(512) 444-3644

WASHINGTON

PRIMA MEXICO
68 Madison
Seattle, WA 98104
(206) 682-6294

INTERIOR DESIGNERS

CARR-WIT
3267 Bee Caves Road #107
Austin, TX 78746
(512) 370-9663

SUSAN DUPÉPÉ
112 W. San Francisco #314
Santa Fe, NM 87501
(505) 982-4536

MARC FIRESTONE
2843 S. Bayshore Drive
Coconut Grove, FL 33133
(305) 445-2508

ANN JAMES
611 Orchard Avenue
Santa Barbara, CA 93105
(805) 969-4554

KITCHELL INTERIOR
DESIGN
7522 E. McDonald Drive
Scottsdale, AZ 85250
(602) 951-0280

HANK MILAM & ASSOC.
24325 Cimarron Court
Laguna Niguel, CA 92677
(714) 831-6513

O'CARROL, PEPIN &
KUCKLEY
436 W. San Francisco Street
Santa Fe, NM 87501
(505) 983-7055

KAREN VAUGHAN
PRODUCTIONS
227 Coggeshall
Newport, RI 02840
(401) 846-4774

VISIONS DESIGN GROUP
510 Galisteo
Santa Fe, NM 87501
(505) 988-3170

LABEN WINGERT
P.O. Box 2045
Santa Fe, NM 87501
(505) 983-7200

READING

A few of our favorite books about Mexico are listed below.

Colle, Marie Pierre. *Casa Poblana*. Monterrey, Mexico: Museo de Monterrey, 1993.

Cordry, Donald and Dorothy. *Mexican Indian Costumes*. Austin: University of Texas Press, 1968.

Fernandez, Miguel Angel and Victor Ruiz. *Mesa Mexicana*. Mexico City: Grupo Finacero Bancomer, 1993.

Fomento Cultural Banamex, A. C. *El Mueble Mexicano: Historia, Evolucion Y Influencias*. Mexico City: Banamex. A. C., 1985.

Garcini, Ricardo Rendon. *Haciendas de Mexico*. Mexico City: Banamex A. C., 1994.

Garrison, G. Richard, and George Rustay. *Early Mexican Houses*. Stamford, Connecticut: Architectural Book Publishing Co. Inc., 1930; 1990.

Yampolsky, Mariana. *La Casa Que Canta*. Mexico City: SEP, 1982.

MEXICAN BOOK RESOURCES

ALLA
102 W. San Francisco Street
Santa Fe, NM 87501
(505) 988-5416

HOWARD KARNO BOOKS
P.O. Box 2100
Valley Center, CA 92082
(619) 749-2304

MINUTIAE MEXICANA
Mexican ICS
124 Avenue Cota
San Clemente, CA 92672
(714) 492-1257

An old *comoda*, or small cabinet, from Ranch Nonuvoah. Chihuahua, features raised panels decorated with lathe-turned rings of ironwood and inlaid bone. On top rest three miniature Mexican trunks. Collection of Jack and Peggy Calderella.

GLOSSARY

Alacena: Cabinet built into a wall.

Aldaba: Latch; hasp; door knocker.

Arcón: Large, locking trunk.

Armario: Armoire, large wardrobe cabinet with doors.

Banco: Bench.

Banquito: Small bench.

Butaca: Classic armchair of Mexico, featuring leather sling seat.

Batea: Carved wooden bowl.

Baúl: Wooden trunk used for storing clothes and personal belongings.

Bebedero: Hollowed-out log used for feeding livestock.

Caoba: Mahogany—reddish-brown, medium hardness.

Caja: Box.

Cajon: Drawer.

Cajonera: Chest of drawers.

Cama: Bed.

Camapec: Bench-style ranch bed.

Cantera: Stone.

Carpintero: Carpenter.

Cedro: Cedar—fragrant, reddish brown, medium to soft hardness, resistant to insects.

Clavo: Hand-forged nail topped with large round head.

Comoda: Long, low cabinet with drawers and/or doors.

Copete: Crest; top decoration of cabinet.

Corazón de yarín: Heart pine—light to reddish wood.

Escabel: Three-legged milking stool.

Equipale: Indigenous barrel-shaped pigskin and bentwood furniture.

Faldon: Skirt.

Gozne hinge: Snipe hinge.

Hoja: Panel.

Mano: Wooden stick used as a pestle in a *mortero*.

Mesa: Table.

Mesa de altar: Altar table.

Mesa de carnicero: Butcher's table.

Mesa de quesero: Table for making cheese.

Mezquite: Mesquite—a dense and durable hardwood, resistant to insects.

Metate: Flat stone on which maize, *cacao*, and other foods are ground with the aid of a *metlapil*.

Metlapil: Elongated cylindrical stone used for grinding on a *metate*.

Molcajete: Stone bowl used for grinding spices and ingredients.

Molde de azucar: Sugar mold.

Mortero: Hollowed-out wood mortar used to crush grain or coffee.

Parota: A dark brown wood, medium hardness, buoyant.

Patas torneadas: Turned legs.

Petaca: Traveling trunk made of leather.

Petaquilla: Wooden trunk with handles on the ends.

Petate: All-purpose mat of interwoven palm or rushes.

Pila: Hollowed-out stone used for watering livestock.

Postigo: Small opening or panel in a door or window.

Puerta: Door.

Rinconera: Three-legged corner table.

Ropero: Freestanding cabinet for storing clothes.

Sabino: Mexican cypress—fine-grained, yellow to clear white wood, with almost no knots, resistant to insects.

Silla: Chair.

Trastero: Freestanding cabinet for storing food or utensils.

Torneo: Turning on a lathe.

Ventana: Window.

Ventanita: Little window; peephole.

Yugo: Yoke.

Zaguán doors: Large doors with smaller inner door used on a *zaguán*.

PHOTOGRAPHIC CREDITS

Photographs © Karen Witynski unless otherwise noted.

Numbers indicate pages.
Key: T — Top Row
        M — Middle
        B — Bottom
        L — Left
        C — Center
        R — Right

Brewster, Will: 55, 66, 67

Carr, Joe P.: xii-TL; xiii-TR, BL, BR; 130-B

Crawford, Grey: 131

Diehl, Teresa Harb: Cover; xix; 22; 23-TR; 24-TL; 25; 40; 44-B; 62; 72; 73-B; 74; 89; 117; 128

Frerck, Robert/© Robert Frerck/Odyssey: xvi; xvii

Hadley, Greg/ © Greg Hadley: 95

Kenny, Gill: Back Cover-R; Half Title Page; Title Page; Copyright Page; xv-B; xxi-BR; xxvi; xxvii; 5-B; 7-B; 31-L; 32; 37-TR, BC; 44-T; 48; 49; 58; 59; 61; 79; 81; 101; 112; 127; 135

Legrou, Michel: 94

Lotz, Herbert: 37-BL; 69; 93; 104

Medina, Alfonso: xiv

Mitchell, W. Scott: 45; 54-T; 85

Salazar, Rafael: xviii; 27

Vertikoff, Alexander: Back Cover-L; vi; x; xv-TR; xx; xxi-T; xxii; xxiii; xxiv; xxviii; xxix; 3; 5; 6; 11; 12; 16; 21; 23-B; 28; 33; 34; 36; 37-ML; 39; 41; 42; 47; 50; 51; 52; 54-B; 56; 57; 60; 63-B; 64; 68; 70; 71; 75; 76; 77; 82; 83; 84; 87; 88; 92; 96; 99; 103; 108; 111; 113; 119

Witynski, Karen: xii-TR, BL, BR; xiii-TL; 17; 24-B; 26; 30-L; 31-L; 35; 37-TL, TC, MC, MR, BR; 38; 46; 63-T; 73-T; 78; 80; 81; 86; 90; 91; 98; 100; 102; 105; 106; 107; 109; 110; 118; 120; 121; 124; 125; 126; 130-T

Page viii
Courtesy The Mexican Museum

Page 122; 123
Courtesy Alex Tschursin, Foreign Traders

Page 10
Courtesy The National Museum of History, Chapultepec Castle, Mexico.
Photograph: Héctor Herrera

We thank the following publications for their permission to reprint their photographs in our book:

Page 4
Courtesy The Meadows Museum, Gloria Kay Giffords and Ray Pearson
The Art of Private Devotion: Retablo Painting of Mexico

Pages 7-T; 8
Courtesy Editorial Trillas, S.A. de C. V.
Arquitectura Vernácula en México

Page 9
Courtesy Virginia B. de Barrios
Editorial Minutiae Mexicana, S. A. de C. V.
A Guide to Mexican Witchcraft
Photograph: Irmgard Johnson

Pages 15; 18; 19
Courtesy Mariana Yampolsky
La Casa Que Canta, SEP

Pages 30-R; 31-R
Courtesy Marie-Pierre Colle,
Casa Poblana, Museum of Monterrey
Photograph: Ignacio Urquiza

Colophon
The body text, set in Cochin, was originally designed by Parisian artist and engraver Charles Nicolas Cochin in the eighteenth century. Chapter openings and subheads are set in New Amigo Regular and captions are set in Trade Gothic Bold Two.